INTRODUCTION

By Joseph Hansen

In 1939 a dispute broke out in the Socialist Workers Party that eventually spread to the world Trotskyist movement. Of all the internal struggles that have occurred in the Fourth International this one must undoubtedly be considered the most important up to now. The conflict began when an unprincipled bloc of dissident tendencies sought to take over leadership of the party on the basis of organizational grievances (alleged "bureaucratic conservatism" of James P. Cannon). To these grievances were added political differences that arose over the Stalin-Hitler pact and the Soviet invasion of Poland and then Finland. In view of these events, Max Shachtman was of the opinion that unconditional defense of the Soviet Union was no longer tenable. James Burnham, a logical positivist and opponent of dialectical materialism, began questioning the correctness of designating the Soviet state as proletarian. The debate extended to the basic philosophical positions of Marxism, as Trotsky, responding to the views of James Burnham and Max Shachtman, took up the relevancy of dialectical materialism to the party's political positions.

The struggle was unusually sharp because of the obvious response inside the Socialist Workers Party to the war pressure. The propaganda machines of the allied powers had taken full advantage of Stalin's maneuvers, and had mounted an anti-Soviet campaign that had telling effect among intellectual circles, including those that had been sympathetic to Trotskyism. Against this pressure, and against its reflection inside the party, the majority insisted on the validity of the policy of revolutionary defense of the Soviet Union against imperialism, whether German or Allied.

The majority documents (and several key minority statements) in this factional struggle are readily available, having been assembled in Leon Trotsky's *In Defense of Marxism* and James P. Cannon's *The Struggle for a Proletarian Party.* These have long been used as textbooks in the Trotskyist movement internationally.

For educational purposes, it would have been useful to reproduce the entire discussion; but the costs were prohibitive for our small organization. Thus many contributions on special points, including the following two articles, have long been out of print.

I wrote "Organizational Methods and Political Principles" while I was with Trotsky in Coyoacan. (With the exception of some stays in New York, I had been there since the first week of September 1937.) Knowing that it would cause a sharp reaction from Abern and that it might be thought to have been inspired by Trotsky because of the place in which it was written, I gave Trotsky the draft as it stood at that point (I intended to work on it some more), and asked him for any suggestions.

I expected that he might go over it in a week or so—when he found an opening in his work schedule. But he gave it back to me within an hour. He appeared pleased. "An excellent article. Very good." To my surprise, he did not have a single criticism, not even a suggestion on changing a sentence or formulation. He took it for granted that it would be sent forthwith for publication in the *Internal Bulletin,* and I did not waste any time mailing it off.

Trotsky, I suppose, favored the article because it was the first contribution in the factional struggle to single out Abern for attack. It is possible, too, that it happened to fit in with a step he had been weighing. In the following two weeks he wrote an article that hit like a bomb in the factional struggle: "A Petty-Bourgeois Opposition in the Socialist Workers Party." (See *In Defense of Marx-*

ism, pp. 108–135 [2011 printing].) In this article, in which he set forth the real issues in dispute and characterized the tendencies, Trotsky referred to what I had written: "I will not go into the historical sequence of the faction fight, referring the reader to the in every respect excellent article by Joseph Hansen, 'Organizational Methods and Political Principles.'"

Today, in 1972, many of the allusions in the articles are obscure. Figures in and around the Trotskyist movement that were well-known thirty-three years ago have died or drifted out of politics. Scandals under heated discussion in the corridors at the time have been forgotten. To explain all these obscure points would require an article much longer than the original. Those wishing to check further will find James P. Cannon's *History of American Trotskyism* and *The Struggle for a Proletarian Party* helpful.

Following the publication of "Organizational Methods and Political Principles" in the *Internal Bulletin*, Abern and Shachtman opened a counterattack. This consisted of passing the word that I was a "liar." In reply I wrote "The Abern Clique." In this I presented evidence to show that I had not lied. Neither Abern nor Shachtman made any retractions. On the other hand they did not repeat their denunciations. And not a single member of their faction attempted a rebuttal.

"The Abern Clique" deals with a specific clique that existed in the early days of the American Trotskyist movement. As a case study it is incomplete; it does not cover the origin of the clique or its subsequent fate. Nonetheless it offers material that may still be instructive in considering the problem of cliquism in the revolutionary movement.

To understand cliquism, it is necessary to begin with the fact that a revolutionary Marxist party is not monolithic. Its ranks, coming from various sectors of the working class, are unevenly developed. This unevenness may be further increased by the recruitment of persons of petty-bourgeois origin in process of becoming proletarianized. Actions engaged in by the party, while raising the general political level among the ranks, can also sharpen the differentiations, since the various sectors of the party become involved in different ways and to different degrees, most often determined by local circumstances. Among other things, teams of unusual effectiveness may form as a result of working closely together in difficult situations or during sharp outbreaks of the class struggle. Friendships formed in such circumstances can prove to be very enduring.

All this is perfectly normal. Through common experience and common study, the party seeks to overcome the unevenness in development among the ranks by converting raw members into seasoned cadres. The true strength of a revolutionary party is measured by its capacity to produce cadres—men and women capable of serving as the general staff of a socialist revolution.

Teams that have displayed special capacities generally serve as models in the party. The condition for this should, however, be noted well. They serve as models only so long as they clearly advance the party's general political positions. If they do not do this, if they come to feel that they constitute a special group, if they try to advance the interests of this special group against the interests of the party as a whole, then the nature of the group turns into its opposite—it becomes a clique. Moreover it can degenerate still further and be lost to the revolutionary movement.

Such a change follows a rather broad dialectical pattern. An impressive example is to be found in Trotsky's balance sheet on the Bolshevik experience with guerrilla war in Russia. The fighting detachments, which engaged in "exemplary actions" in the 1905–07 Russian revolution, conducted themselves at first in model fashion. As the revolutionary wave receded, however, they began to "misbehave," to descend to "bandit attacks of the most ordinary criminal type." Even the most disciplined detachments degenerated. "Always having large sums of money, the fighters began to preoccupy themselves with carousing, in the course of which they fell into the hands of the police. Thus, little by little, the entire fighting detachment came to an ignominious end." (See *Stalin* by Leon Trotsky, pp. 95–99.)

The history of the revolutionary-socialist movement contains innumerable examples of cliquism. A clique need not begin with a "heroic" period. It may consist of members with little in the way of a distinguished service record. Mutual grievances, real or imaginary, hold them together. Mere congeniality may be the cement.

Cliquism is most serious when it appears at a

leadership level. The Industrial Workers of the World (IWW) suffered from the "headquarters gang," as did the Socialist Party in the time of Eugene V. Debs. And the Communist Party in the early days was rife with cliquism. (See *The First Ten Years of American Communism* by James P. Cannon.)

At bottom, cliquism in a revolutionary party reflects the pressure of the surrounding capitalist society. When the going is tough, when the objective difficulties seem insuperable, when the party is under heavy attack, when setbacks occur, pessimism and demoralization can set in. A tendency to withdraw from what appear to be fruitless battles can arise. Some sectors of the party are certain to be more affected than others—again because of the unevenness in the composition of the party, differences in origin of its components, different experiences, varying capacities of local leaders, and so on. Such moods favor the appearance of cliques that come to believe that the true source of the party's lack of progress must lie in the leadership or in the program.

One of the curiosities of cliques is their inability to see the similarity between their form of struggle and one of the most repellent features of capitalist institutions; that is, an internal life governed by warring, power-hungry groups whose concerns include anything but upholding principles.

It is unfortunate that in the minds of most members of the Socialist Workers Party the name of Martin Abern is associated only with the role he played in the 1939–40 struggle. Yet he deserves to be remembered more favorably. He was one of the pioneers of American Communism and of American Trotskyism.

He was born December 25, 1898. He worked his way through high school and enrolled in the University of Minnesota. On the campus he was a popular figure, as might be expected from the fact that he was a star quarterback on the football team. But he was also known as a dedicated socialist. In 1912, at the age of fourteen, he had joined the Young People's Socialist League in Minneapolis; and in 1915 he joined the Socialist Party, later becoming the Local Secretary.

Although he was known in the Minneapolis movement as a "born recruiter," he evidently wanted more action than could be found in the Social Democracy. In 1916 he joined the IWW. This was not incompatible with membership in the Socialist Party and in fact it was common among left wingers in those days to hold cards in both organizations.

When the United States entered the first world war, the left-wing Socialists sought to build an antiwar movement. However they had neither a correct theory nor a good model to help them in this. Their policy consequently was to oppose the imperialist war by refusing to register in the draft.

Martin Abern was indicted by the federal government and served a six-month prison term in Minnesota for this "crime." After being released he was still subjected to harassment by the federal authorities, and was indicted once more for his opposition to the war.

Deep rifts had appeared in the Socialist Party over what attitude to take toward the war. The Russian revolution in 1917 deepened the divisions and created new ones. In Minnesota, Abern participated in organizing the left wing contingent there in anticipation of the September 1919 convention of the Socialist Party. At that convention the left wing delegations split away to form the Communist Labor Party. Abern thus became one of the founding members of that organization.

In 1919–20 Abern served as District Organizer of the Minnesota Communist Party. In May 1920, at the first underground convention of the Communist Party, held at Bridgeman, Michigan, he was elected to the Central Executive Committee. At the age of twenty-two, he was its youngest member. Later he served for a time on the Political Committee. Among the reasons for this swift recognition were Abern's dedication, his efficiency, his capacity to handle details and his doggedness in seeing that decisions were carried out.

He was the first person to fill the post of National Secretary of the Young Workers League (which later became the Young Communist League), remaining until 1923.

In 1922, at the age of twenty-four, he was a delegate to the Fourth World Congress of the Communist International. He was also a delegate to the Third World Congress of the Young Communist International.

From 1924 to 1926 he served as District Organizer and Organizational Secretary of the Workers (Communist) Party, Chicago district.

Later he became Assistant National Secretary of the International Labor Defense, the organization headed by James P. Cannon that gained world renown for its successes in mobilizing mass support for Sacco and Vanzetti, Mooney and Billings, and other political prisoners.

When Cannon in 1928 returned from the Sixth World Congress of the Communist International, he brought back a copy of a document that had been submitted by Trotsky for consideration by the delegates, *The Draft Program of the Communist International: A Criticism of Fundamentals*. This was the document that won Cannon to the cause of Trotsky, then in exile in Alma Ata. Cannon showed it first to his companion, Rose Karsner, and then to his closest co-workers Martin Abern, and Max Shachtman. Trotsky's critique won them as it had Cannon.

The Lovestone-Wolfe majority leadership of the Communist Party was doing its utmost at the time to curry favor with Stalin. As soon as this leadership got wind of the fact that Trotsky's document was being circulated, they moved against the incipient faction. On October 27, 1928, Cannon, a member of the Political Committee; Abern, a member of the Central Executive Committee; and Shachtman, an alternate to the Central Executive Committee, were expelled on charges of "Trotskyism." The three replied by carrying their fight to the public, recording it in the pages of *The Militant*, the first issue of which was dated November 15, 1928. And at a conference held in Chicago May 17–19, 1929, they and others like Vincent R. Dunne, Carl Skoglund, and Arne Swabeck, launched the Communist League of America (Opposition). That was how the American Trotskyist movement was founded.

With a background like that how could Abern have ended up as he did? The answer is not simple, but I think it can be found in three circumstances.

1. In the beginning, the American Trotskyist movement consisted of 100 to 200 members. Finances were extremely limited. To even bring out *The Militant* regularly was a continual problem that often mounted to a crisis level. The small movement was slandered, hounded, and persecuted from all sides, one of the worst sources being the Stalinized Communist Party. Under these conditions it was extremely difficult to prevent the group from turning inward and devouring itself, no matter what the quality of the leadership.

2. Most of these Trotskyist cadres had been formed in the factional jungle of the Communist Party in the twenties, and not all of them succeeded in overcoming this training. Abern was one of those who continued using methods that were considered normal in the early days of the Communist Party (and in the Socialist Party before it).

3. For reasons that remain obscure, Abern developed an extremely subjective attitude toward Cannon. His dislike and even hatred of Cannon were of such proportions that they affected his political judgment in internal party affairs. It became an obsession with him to overturn the "regime."

In view of this it is understandable, if not excusable, why he took the position he did in the 1939–40 factional struggle. The opportunity to downgrade if not displace Cannon came first in his thinking. Burnham's hostility to dialectical materialism did not appear to Abern to be of major consequence—he probably considered Burnham to be more of a peripheral figure than a Trotskyist cadre. Shachtman's shift on the defense of the Soviet Union likewise did not appear to him to be of decisive importance. Most likely Shachtman would in time reverse himself. Moreover, Shachtman did not have a firm base among the cadres; his real role was to serve as an attorney for others. Besides which Shachtman himself had come to share Abern's views on the "regime," at least on the need to "cut down Cannon." Abern thus saw no good reason why he should not make a combination with Burnham and Shachtman. It was a fatal political error, the logic of which brought him to split from the Socialist Workers Party and participate in setting up a rival organization, the Workers Party, although he had no differences with the program of the Fourth International.

The unprincipled combination soon began to come apart. Burnham left within weeks, proclaiming his theory that a "new class" had appeared in the Soviet Union, the "managers," and that this new class was taking over on a world scale, not least of all in the United States. Shachtman shortly announced his conversion to a caricature of Burnham's view; that is, that the Stalinist regime in the Soviet Union represented "bureaucratic collectivism."

Abern's followers themselves began to divide. Part of them, in collaboration with various recruits to the Workers Party, became convinced that the socio-economic structure of the Soviet Union was "state capitalist." At the same time, they revised their hostile estimate of the Socialist Workers Party, considering it now to represent the only proletarian revolutionary party in the United States. In 1947 they rejoined the Socialist Workers Party as an organized grouping, the Johnson-Forest tendency.

By this time Abern had become rather inactive in the Workers Party, perhaps because of a worsening heart condition. However, in 1948, he attended a public meeting in New York sponsored by the Socialist Workers Party. It was the commemoration of Trotsky's death or possibly the celebration of the November 1917 Russian revolution. Rose Karsner greeted him and they talked at length. Karsner saw him again once or twice and reported that he was considering rejoining the party.

Whether he would have eventually done this, whether he had come to realize how mistaken his course had been in 1939–40 and before, are questions that cannot be answered. On April 28, 1949, at the age of fifty, he died of a heart attack.

One of the outcomes of the 1939–40 struggle was a settlement of accounts with Abern as a cliquist. That record will continue to serve as educational material in the Socialist Workers Party. But we should not permit knowledge of Abern's other side to be lost.

He understood the importance of efficient administration, of carrying through on details, of assuming responsibility for jobs that others considered to be mere drudgery and beneath their dignity. What was most attractive about him was his interest in comrades as human beings and his concern for them when they ran into difficulties. This personal warmth, which helped make him a "born recruiter" in his youth, finally turned into a disadvantage in his case; it was one of the things that held his following together.

Trotsky was well aware of Abern's positive side. It led him to observe to us on one occasion in Coyoacan when we were talking about Abern that it is necessary to include that kind, too, in the party leadership.

JUNE 24, 1972

ORGANIZATIONAL METHODS AND POLITICAL PRINCIPLES

By Joseph Hansen

Turning organizational considerations upside down

To those comrades who have become part of our movement since the entry into the Socialist Party and who are now attempting to arrive at a serious and well-considered understanding of the political and organizational differences which are being discussed in our party, some of the aspects of the present struggle over the Russian question are very perplexing.

Especially perplexing is the force of attraction which has temporarily bound together the different political groups of the Minority. How can those who advocate defeatism in the USSR unite with those who don't know where they stand now or where they will jump tomorrow? How can these two groups unite with a third which votes for defense of the USSR and thus agrees with the political opponents of the Majority?

The motives which impelled the third group under the leadership of Comrade Abern to join the variegated Minority more than any other single factor cause serious comrades to wonder, since Comrade Abern is one of those who like Comrades Cannon and Shachtman and Comrade Spector of Canada helped found the Left Opposition in America and hence should know and be following the principles of Marxism. Comrade Abern (with his friends, naturally) is the only one in the Minority who up to date has declared his agreement with the political position of the Majority and the only one who separates himself from supporting the Majority position solely because of *organizational* reasons. How can this action of Comrade Abern be squared with the fundamental Marxist principle he presumably would follow that organizational concessions may be made for the sake of political agreement but never political concessions for the sake of organizational agreement? Comrade Abern's action can easily lead one to believe that there must be more than lies on the surface, that he is following some basic principle, has some highly important end in view, which requires this devious combination and hence is worthy of support. Perhaps Comrade Abern hopes through an organizational bloc with political opponents to keep the party better on the rails of the Majority political position with which he agrees. Perhaps Comrade Abern hopes after the victory of the Minority bloc to have gained sufficient weight in his own right to wield the organizational blackjack on his erstwhile organizational allies if they raise their principled differences with the basic principles of the Fourth International.

In the internal struggles of the party as well as in other fields, the experience of the past can help in solving the problems of the present. Comrade Abern's role in the present struggle might better be appreciated if we recall the role that was played by various elements at the time of the struggle over entry into the Socialist Party. In that fight, Comrade Abern's perspective was a highly *conservative* perspective, *the most conservative in the party,* although that, true enough, did not prevent it from entailing the most drastic organizational conclusions. Comrade Abern opposed the entry not on principled grounds, as he quite frankly stated, but on tactical grounds. He agreed apparently with all the political conclusions of those who advocated entry. He maintained that it was merely a question of what organizational methods we should use in accomplishing our task of influencing the development of the Socialist Party and that we could do it, even with our small forces, more successfully from the outside. So far as I know he has not changed that estimate to this day. Yet despite the fact that Comrade Abern had only tactical differences, he planned quite deliberately to split from the party if he did not succeed in gaining the majority for his *conservative* organizational position. And he cited as justification that there are times when a split is justified over tactical considerations. All the members of his faction (known as the Muste-Abern faction) were carefully prepared for the eventuality of split. Thus Comrade Abern found *his* organizational methods so *rigid*, so *inflexible*, and so *conservative* that he was brought to the very brink of the extremely *adventuristic political position* of splitting from the Fourth International. He exchanged conservative politics for adventurism, and adaptable organizational methods for intransigeance. Then as now Comrade Abern placed organizational methods above political principles.

Up to the very time of the convention of the Workers Party which decided upon entry, Comrade Abern had not made up his mind whether to carry through the planned split or not. As he informed those of us who adhered at that time to his position, split depended solely upon the size of the forces which opposed the entry. If they were large the split would be carried through; if they were small then the split would not be carried through. Split hinged on counting heads. Such a position could not help but cover up the alien tendency of Oehler and contribute to his making greater gains than he would have made otherwise since Oehler made the entry a principled question and split on *principled* grounds. Many adherents of the Muste-Abern faction decided that entry was a principled question if it was a splitting question as Abern claimed and joined the Oehlerites. Of the various organizational schools in our party, that of Comrade Abern's has proved to be one of the most costly.

The miserable end of Comrade Abern's anti-entry faction is well worth considering in the light of the present struggle. Comrade Weber had the political courage to break sharply from the incorrect position he had taken in supporting Abern and this had a powerful influence in disintegrating the faction. After alarming defections to the Oehlerites on one side and the Cannon-Shachtman entry faction on the other, a leading comrade labeled quite modestly the "Lenin of America"* came down from Canada to save the pieces, but neither his organizational methods nor his political principles proved more efficient than Comrade Abern's. A bloc of Stalinist stooges left with appropriate fanfare in the *Daily Worker.*

Comrade Abern succeeded only in gaining the organizational recompense of placing some of his faction members on the National Committee—the "Lenin of America," A. J. Muste, himself, and Gerry Allard who later found it more profitable to sacrifice his political principles for the sake of exercising his organizational efficiency as editor of Norman Thomas' pious mouthpiece, *The Call.*

A. J. Muste, titular head of the faction who had been ballyhooed as the best organizational find since the inception of the Left Opposition in the United States, later found it more profitable to utilize his organization efficiency in the service of Christ and a quiet chapel. Vereecken and Sneevliet in Europe who had lent their prestige and authority to the anti-entry position also ended miserably, finding organizational solace in the enemy camp of the London Bureau. Out in California, Barney Moss—West Coast lieutenant of Abern—retired to the academic Berkeley hillsides, far from political work and care, after he broke once and for all with Bolshevik organizational methods, and now spends his time under the eucalyptus trees browbeating the youth who are attracted by his sherry wine and guff.

True, Comrade Abern cannot be held responsible for the renegacy of these ex-members of the Fourth International, but it is not without significance that all of the leaders of the anti-entry faction except Comrade Weber, who broke demonstratively and acknowledged his error, placed organizational efficiency above political principles and ended in various camps opposed to the Fourth International.

A party may have highly efficient organizational methods, and yet be an executioner of the socialist revolution as the Stalinist party. A party may have inefficient organizational methods and be reformist as the Socialist Party or the Lovestoneites. A

* At the present time, I understand, this "Lenin of America" spends his time contemplating the navel of a phonograph record.

party may have the most expensive stream-lining in the way of organizational methods and yet be the most reactionary party in the world, as the party of Hitler. And a party may have highly efficient organizational methods or very slipshod methods and yet be a revolutionary workers' party. In the one case its successes will be *more* marked, and its growth *more* rapid and sure, other factors being equal. But for Marxists the first thing to decide upon is not the *efficiency* of an organization but its *political* principles: are they correct ones that will lead the working class to socialism or are they false and dangerous? If one considers a given set of political principles to be the ones the revolutionary party of the workers must follow, then—and only then—does he consider their organizational application and the relative efficiency which can be obtained from them in a given situation. *Political principles come first.*

Organizational methods and administrative efficiency

Just as the more conscious followers of Abern place organizational methods above political principles, so the newcomers to their ranks place administrative efficiency above organizational methods. Consequently there is a whole series of gradations of sub-political motivations that have drawn these people together and will hold them together until they learn better or else fall into the state of arrested political development which seems to characterize some of our otherwise capable and loyal comrades. Someone's letter wasn't answered; someone didn't like the tone of voice or manners of this or that leader on some particular occasion; someone walking down the street with a leader was afraid to break a silence he felt to be intentionally oppressive; someone found the floors of the headquarters unswept, or the desk without stamps for an important mailing; someone foolishly came on time to an appointment—at worst fanciful, but even granting all these accusations to be true (and the Minority members sin as much in this as those of the Majority) still all this is only secondary to the problem of deciding upon the correct organizational methods to fit the political principles of the party. Thus the launching of the campaign technique was an organizational method to better implement our ideas, and while there is no sharp break in this field of the party's life just as there is no sharp break between organizational and political problems and one grades into another (in a very acute revolutionary situation any of these can assume *principled* proportions—but clearly declared to be of principled importance *not* just organizational), yet getting the handbills out in time, seeing that squads distribute them, paying a deposit to hold a hall for a lecture—all this can be classified as within the administrative sphere.

The imagination to conceive changing our whole organizational form from independence to organizational amalgamation with and subordination to a larger party and to accomplish this successfully despite bitterest and most conservative opposition from all sides, this is imagination of high organizational caliber—or more prosaically, it is Bolshevism. The sending out of the mail telling the comrades when and where, this is administrative—still administrative if not carried out at all or no matter how nicely the letters were made up or how carefully they were addressed so that they got to the right people and not to an alien force.

Let us not confuse an administrative job with an organizational method or a political principle.

Correct organizational methods are of paramount importance as the history of our party in the United States shows and they have loomed high—far higher in my estimation than all of Abern's undoubted administrative ability. It is all the more inexcusable then to place efficient administration above organizational methods. Of what use is the efficient administration of inefficacious organizational methods?

First come political principles, then organizational methods, and only after that the question of efficient administration.

You comrades in the Minority, where does your caucus differ so fundamentally in its position or so conspicuously in the successes of its leaders from that of the Majority on the *administrative* plane that you find it impossible to join the Majority in the fight for correct political principles and correct organizational methods in our party?

Are the administrative records of the Minority leaders so outstanding, are they such models of orderliness, such technicians, so thorough, prompt, dynamic, machine-like and disciplined that you must perforce take over their political and organizational revision, casting aside the basic doctrines of the Fourth International and the organizational methods which have played a major role in building our section into the most powerful in the Fourth International?

Some organizational methods

For the moment let us leave aside the political differences which separate the Defeatist and the Doubtist sections of the Minority from the basic position of the Fourth International and consider the organizational accusations which are concentrated most sharply in the position of Comrade Abern.

First, it must be stated that most of the accusations which are now being made are not new. They did not burst from cover full-feathered in the last two or three months. Secondly, it must be added that the greater part of the accusations, although generally known throughout the party and quite freely discussed by everyone, are of the type which in letters follow the heading "personal" and which avoid expression in resolutions, documents, or even speeches at official meetings where they could be met squarely. This is one of the organizational methods unfortunately prevalent in certain circles of our party.

The Oehlerites based a good deal of their appeal to the membership not so much on the merits of the "French turn" and its American application as upon the organizational trick of endless hammering upon a few catchwords: "Cannon hatchetmen," "Cannon stooges," and "Philadelphia thugs." A newcomer could not help being impressed by these cries—where there was so much noise there must be some blood. The victim of this organizational procedure began to interpret every action of the leadership—no matter what—as a plot, deep and double-dyed, against the rank and file and the free development of political personalities who might challenge their clutch upon alleged bureaucratic sinecures. The repetition of some of these Oehlerite catchwords in a quieter and milder organizational form by some of the adherents of the Abern-Muste caucus lent weight to them. Cannon's organizational methods were "notorious;" Cannon did not solve problems by political persuasion but by "bureaucratic repressions;" "Cannon wanted a 'one-man party'; etc., etc. All these epithets found their most literary expression I believe in California where Symes-Clement-Rogers took them over whole and undigested as a slick organizational method and repeated them with that peculiar nervous frenzy which characterized the Clarityite caucus in California.

"We agree with you politically ninety-nine and forty-four hundreths percent," Symes insisted over and over during the Good and Welfare period of the branch meetings she attended; "in fact in many respects we are better Trotskyites than you—but . . . we can't agree with your organizational methods. Bolshevism leads to Stalinism and Cannon is a son-of-a-bitch. Just wait until Shachtman gets here. He'll straighten Cannon out." (Symes didn't wait long enough.) This language of course was unlady-like even for Symes, but any of the California comrades who battled her attempts at revising our program can vouch for the literal accuracy of this quotation in its entirety. Whoever supported the position of the Fourth International in California was dubbed by Symes a "Cannon hatchetman," a "Cannon stooge." It was difficult to believe in listening to her that the Oehlerite and entry fights had ended, especially when Symes made overtures to the ex-members of the Muste-Abern caucus. Rogers ended up calling the cops; Clement didn't count much as an independent political factor—he was only Symes husband—and Symes returned where she had started, gnashing her teeth in *The Call,* berating Trotskyism as "inverted Stalinism" and peddling the pathetic and wornout wares of Angelica Balabanoff.

On the international scale this same organizational method of fighting the Bolshevik line is pursued by Pivert and Co. against the Fourth International in general and Comrade Trotsky in particular. That this argument could arise again in *our* ranks is perhaps explainable in view of the newness of many comrades. That it could be repeated by old experienced comrades with the hope that it would take in anyone who has been in the ranks a few years is rather amazing. In any event the record of this particular organizational method is not only worn in the grooves but just a trifle cracked. It is simply not true that whoever arrives at the same conclusions as are recorded in the basic documents of the Fourth International is a stooge or a hatchetman for some particular leader.

The positive side of this organizational method

In contrast to the "hatchetmen" and "stooges" the party is blessed with the "independent thinkers," who constitute the other side of the coin. Independent thinkers in this case are those who arrive at a position different from certain leaders and in agreement with other leaders. This of course is a neat and useful distinction—very efficient organizationally. One not only is free to support certain leaders without his conscience accusing him of being a "stooge" but he enjoys a certain eminence, an independence of personality (which of course has nothing to do with "American individuality") and that is no mean qualification in these times when Marx, Engels, Lenin, and Trotsky have dug up so much ground previously. Let us finish with this argument once and for all. Even the bourgeois professors prove often enough (in peace times) that the grain of originality in anyone is strictly limited; as for the Marxists, they are more interested in politics.

In the present struggle, the epithet, "independent thinkers," is merely a clever organizational stunt designed for morale and used by certain factionalists to pat themselves and their followers on the back. I have yet to hear of a single case in our movement where any one with a new idea or a new formulation of an old idea was stifled, gagged, prevented from presenting it in either the party press or internal bulletin, or driven from the ranks to waste away his talents a mute and inglorious revolutionary Milton.

A subdivision of the "independent thinkers" designed to influence the youth movement organizationally is the "persecuted youth." These are merely the "independent thinkers" who belong to the youth—organizationally—and who suffer from the alleged bureaucratic repressions of the party regime. Some of these youth have been in the revolutionary movement as long as fifteen or sixteen years, long enough to no longer look convincing as suffering choir boys. The wear and tear on their mimeograph machines as a mute evidence of their organizational methods should alone prove that far from suffering from repression they are not repressed enough.

The argument of the "persecuted youth" is one of the most shallow and demagogic of all. Its appeal is directed to the *leaders* of the youth organization. Those thoroughly capable rank and file youth members who are treading on the heels of these leaders receive a colder and more hostile appreciation. A sharp and salutary break with the hidebound organizational conservatism in this section of our movement would prove far more valuable to the youth than the organizational method of thumping them a thousand and one times between the shoulder blades and teaching them self-pity.

'Inside dope'—the underground organizational method

The well-known fact that the National Office is far from being a model of efficiency in such administrative matters as promptly answering letters from comrades in the field (I speak particularly of the past) has acted as a catalyst in precipitating a grouping in our party which lives on the "inside dope." Someone high in the party flashes all the pertinent inner news involving the most authoritative bodies of the party to his personal friends, even though they may not sit upon so much as a Branch executive, and they in turn enjoy the aura of always being in the "know," acquainted with all the "important dope" in the Political Committee. It is absolutely elementary that only the Political Committee as a whole has the right to pass out information of concern to it unless serious political differences arise which require the intervention of the membership—there is no other way of protecting the party not only from enemy forces but from disturbances which are not important enough to warrant attention and energy from the ranks. Why then the organizational method of the grapevine? It is a distinct flattery to be in such close connection with the center even though it must be kept sub rosa since the information does not come through the normal party channels. The comrade who falls for this (as I once did) feels superior to the other rank and filers, smarter, and something of a leader in being able to anticipate the mimeograph of the National Office by a few days. This organizational method alone is basis enough for the crystallization of a kind of grouping which springs to the defense of its main-root when a faction fight threatens, which might have organizational consequences against the channels of their information. But it is highly damaging to the political development of a newcomer to this school. He learns to depend on letters from the center instead of his own judgment. He learns the cynical contempt toward the other party leaders which characterizes his mentor. The authority of the party and its leading bodies is lowered to a point where observance of discipline in action becomes desultory. The grapevine is one organizational method which should be condemned in our party. For greater administrative efficiency in our National Office, yes—even if we have to draft a few more stenographers into service; but an end to the sieve from the top which spreads the "inside dope."

The empiric school of riddles

The organizational accusation of the Defeatists and the Doubtists—that the regime bases itself conservatively on the fundamental conceptions of the Fourth International—this of course flows from their principled position. The Defeatists want an organization that will express *their political principles* efficiently (defeatism in Russia, loose party organization, part time functionaries, etc.); the Doubtists want an organization that will express *their doubts* efficiently. Thus there is a very sharp cleavage in the theoretical positions back of the organizational grievances which have temporarily united the Minority. None of them like the regime of the Majority for entirely different reasons. Comrade Abern has not yet given theoretical expression to his organizational views, perhaps because he agrees with the political position of the Majority. Apparently he has succeeded in divorcing theory from practise with one hundred percent administrative efficiency.

Inasmuch as the organizational conclusions of the Defeatists and the Doubtists are the result of theoretical positions at variance with the present position of the party, their arguments are of much greater weight and importance than the arguments of those in the Abern position who are attempting to lift themselves in the party by nothing but their administrative bootstraps. For the first time in our movement we have a school of riddlemakers.

Beginning with the question, "What do you tell the Polish workers when the Red Army crosses the frontier?" the school of answering problems with riddles has expanded even more rapidly than the "imperialist" empire of Alexander the Great, taking in Persia and Afghanistan in a few days and then in one leap, India ("answer yes or no" in the most formal categoric style of British empiricism) but unlike the "imperialism" of Alexander, this school did not stop at India. When a representative of Ceylon came to America, the riddlemakers warm-heartedly made up a sparkingly fresh and original riddle right on the spot: "What do you tell the Ceylonese workers if the Red Army crosses the frontier into Ceylon?" And when a representative came from China, they again showed their originality by marching the Red Army promptly across the Chinese frontier. As yet no representative of the Fourth International has appeared from Alaska or we might expect these independent thinkers to freeze a bridge of ice over Bering Straits for the convenience of a Red Army on skates—in brief since the western border of Canada is unfortunately not fortified—"What do you tell the American workers if the Red Army invades California?" This in the minds of the independent thinkers of the Minority looms more important than the question of just what they would tell the American workers if their faction took over the Socialist Workers Party.

In place of serious analysis based on the actual concrete class forces warring on the world arena, the Minority have cooked up a never ending series of riddles with glib and independently thought out variations. When it is pointed out that we never defended each and every action of the Red Army any more than we did of the G.P.U. or of Stalin's diplomatic corps, or his 13th Street hacks, or his trade union flunkeys—that we defend the Soviet Union with our own methods and our own forces regardless of what Stalin does or does not do, the Minorityites dropped back to the second line trenches. "But there is terrible danger that Stalin will gain control over the Indian revolution." Yes—there is terrible danger, and we fight it, but that does not change our estimate of the economic conquests of October or our defense of these conquests. There was terrible danger in the United States that Stalinism would conquer the C.I.O. but that did not lead us to posing the question of revising our fundamental analysis of the U.S.S.R. To raise that question now because Stalinism is a danger in the colonial countries (and more acutely in view of the coming revolutions) makes one wonder what we are dealing with—political virgins who are first now realizing what Stalinism means and how we fight it?

Now the third line trenches of the Minority are opening their guns. "Would it not be better to overthrow the Soviet Economy for the sake of overthrowing Stalin?" Thus some of the Minority comrades are beginning to ask, "Would it not be better to destroy the degenerated workers' state and replace it even with fascism for the sake of destroying Stalin?" As if the ghastly experience of Italy and Germany were not bitter enough! This is the bridge where the Minority meets those who hold there is no difference between Fascism and Communism. And that also is the parade ground of the imperialist democratic warmongers.

The riddle of the riddlemakers is not difficult to solve. They arose in an organizational way as an attempt to pose embarrassing questions which would stump the conservative leadership with problems "unheard of in their philosophy" of Marxism particularly in "*this* concrete war" and which would provide an opening wedge for the Minority comrades to introduce their political position as the official position of the party. The Minorityites hoped to prove their contention that the Majority is bureaucratic, conservative, "inept," ("tail-endist" to revive the more colorful phrase that was used by Abern and Muste in the entry fight) through posing questions which the Majority, according to the blue-print, would fumble. The cost of teaching their membership the facile method of riddlemaking instead of concrete analysis based on actual forces of course did not enter into their calculations. That cost, like all the costs of mis-education, is to be borne by those who were not yet experienced enough to see the organizational reason for the sudden manufacture of riddles.

Why did the riddlemakers come to the front in this particular struggle? Even without considering Burnham's withdrawn resolution it is not difficult to see that the Minority is weighted down on the side away from Marxism—the side that hinges its judgment upon each concrete event in and of itself and divorced from its historical and class relationship. Is this concrete act good or bad? Is it an imperialist act or isn't it an imperialist act? The fixed and iron categories are set up and each event shoved into its pigeonhole sheared clean of all conflicting forces, all shifting, mobile, and temporary factors. "It's an 'imperialist' act," and the act is shoved once and for all into the imperialist pigeonhole. On a wider scale, Professor Dewey gave a good demonstration of this philosophical school of thought when in a recent issue of the Sunday New York Times he stated categorically that the concrete experience of the Russian revolution had shown that the way of violent revolutionary change could not better human relations. In brief—all of Bolshevism and the titanic experience of October spawned only Stalinism. Unfortunately for Professor Dewey's philosophy, revolutions will continue to occur in the future just as they have in the past, whether individual philosophers think they are best or not, and it is *this* kind of concrete ground from which the Marxists start. Aside from that, if Professor Dewey did not enjoy high standing, a comfortable salary, and congenial friends in the professorial world, but starved in the ranks of the working class and the unemployed, he might change his mind about the benefits of revolution—and revolution in the *Bolshevik* style. The philosophical school of Pragmatism of which Professor Dewey is the acknowledged head, is the prevailing philosophy in America, the practical, humdrum, work-a-day concrete handmaid of idealism. To the American Marxists this school of philosophy is a bitter enemy. When it penetrates our ranks it must be fought and counteracted even in those times when it does not raise political differences with the line of Marxism. That is a task far more difficult and serious than the composition of riddles.

Will you defend the Soviet Union if Stalin attacks it with the Red Army?

Our basic conception of the Soviet Union to date has rested on our analysis of its economy. Taking as our starting point the key question for Communists at all times—the question of private property in the means of production, we decided long ago that the economy of the Soviet Union was a workers' economy, that it was therefore a mighty positive force for the world revolution and that we would defend it against all attack, subordinating that defense only to the world revolution as indicated in one of the resolutions of the First World

Congress in 1919. During the past years we have defended it against the attack of Stalin no matter what tool he used against that economy, whether the G.P.U., the lies of his journalists, the frame-ups of his judicial apparatus, or the firing squads of the Red Army. We had to differentiate sharply between the economy which was the greatest ally of world revolution within the Soviet Union and the political regime which was based on that economy and yet corroding it. We advocated political revolution against the Stalin regime which meant fighting the Red Army arms in hand if in a revolutionary situation it acted as the instrument of Stalin against the revolutionary workers of the Soviet Union. Arms are the customary weapons of political revolutions and civil wars. (Naturally in our strategy we would attempt to win over the ranks of the Red Army if it were not possible to win the army over as a whole.) On the other hand if Stalin were forced to act in defense of the Soviet Union before that revolutionary situation arrived in Russia, without abating our opposition to his regime in the slightest we would not oppose such actions but would be in the forefront of carrying them out efficiently. The existence of the Soviet economy gives us the touchstone by which to judge whether or not it is still a workers' state, no matter what the deformations. If that economy is crushed then it will be time to declare that it is a capitalist state in which we struggle for social revolution and defeatism in time of war. The only other alternative, that a new form of exploitation hitherto unknown to history has arisen, has been answered by Comrade Trotsky in his article, "The U.S.S.R. in War." Yes, we defend the Soviet Union, not only against Hitler and the democratic imperialists, but against Stalin and his instruments as well.

The character of the war

It is precisely in order to avoid characterizing the actions of the U.S.S.R. in the Marxist way on the basis of the economy and the political regime resting on that economy that the comrades of the Minority have now taken as their touchstone in judging events the character of the war. The war is imperialist, they say, therefore everything that happens in that war is imperialist. The pigeonholes have been cut, the events must fit them. They grant that the character of the war might change, but as to what concrete events would change the character of the war they are conveniently vague.

Thousands of times the quotation of Clausewitz that war is the continuation of politics by other means has been cited in our press and the concrete meaning of its corrollary explained time and time again: the character of a war is determined by the economy of the state which wages war. In our press "imperialism" has come to mean exactly the economy of a state dominated by finance-capitalism, as explained by Comrade O'Rourke in his article in Bulletin No. 3, so that when we say that a war is an imperialist war of conquest we mean by that the war of a finance-capitalist state. A feudal state can wage only a feudal war no matter how much territory it conquers. A slave state can wage only a war characteristic of its economy. A degenerated workers' state can wage only the war of a degenerated workers' state. To use the *general*—not Marxist—meaning of imperialism* in relation to the U.S.S.R. in order to characterize its role as "imperialist" and thus hope to lump it together with the capitalist states is at best a confusion of terms—at worst a cheap trick worthy of a sharp high school debater. The war conducted by the imperialist states is an imperialist war. The war conducted by the U.S.S.R. is the war of a degenerated workers' state. We oppose the degeneration; we defend the workers' state. We start not from our characterization of the war but from our characterization of the state.

Measuring all events by the "character of the war" is a sharp axe with which to cut away the rudder and masts of Marxism. "If Great Britain should attack the Soviet Union now, we would not defend the U.S.S.R.," say the Defeatists. Why? "Because the character of the war has not changed." In other words, the iron category has not been changed by these independent thinkers. Marxists on the contrary seek those dynamic forces moving in the direction opposed to the enemy and defend and support these forces. The war is not *all* imperialist. One very important part of that war (covering one-sixth of the earth's surface!) is

* Imperialism—The policy or practice of seeking to extend the control or empire of a nation.—Webster's Collegiate Dictionary. This definition could apply equally well to the progressive conquests against capitalism by a *healthy* workers' state.

the deadliest enemy of imperialism—the Soviet economy. The world revolution has everything to gain in defending that economy. What can be gained by overthrowing it? That would be about as intelligent and progressive as advocating that Tom Girdler's thugs be allowed to smash the C.I.O. completely, wipe it out of existence with machine guns and tear gas because the policies of Lewis do not fit with those of the Fourth International. No matter what philosophical school we belong to, in politics it is a matter of self-preservation to be able to distinguish allies from enemies.

Yes, war pressure of the imperialist democracies

The imperialist democracies have set up a great hue and cry about the fate of poor imperialist Czechoslovakia, poor imperialist Poland, and now poor imperialist Finland. The condemnation they heap upon the U.S.S.R. does not distinguish in the slightest between the progressive nature of the basic economy and the reactionary nature of Stalin's political regime. In fact the imperialist democrats deliberately confuse them, lump them together, and attempt to brand the workers' revolution as synomous with Stalinism. Against this vicious campaign it is necessary for our movement to wage the sharpest, most relentless struggle. That the Defeatist and Doubtist comrades of the Minority have allowed their analysis of the Soviet Union to take on the same coloration as that of the democrats—dumping everything into one pot—is an alarming symptom in our movement. It is necessary only to recall in conjunction with this similarity in analysis the fact that it arose at the same time as the democratic hue and cry, receives its most agitated and acute expression with every new crisis on the war front. It is not at all the case of calling the Defeatist and Doubtist comrades of the Minority *conscious* reflectors of this war pressure.* But this phenomenon in our party at this time seems more than coincidental, especially in the light of the well-recognized bad social composition of our ranks in the centers of Minority strength. It should call forth from the Defeatists and Doubtists of the Minority the most careful explanation if they wish to avoid the conclusion that seems most natural in the situation.

As for the organizational motivation of Comrade Abern in adhering to the Minority, I should like to read an explanation from him himself. His motives seem far more obscure—or else brazenly obvious.

What will be the political line of the organizational bloc?

Inasmuch as the Minority have the perfect and unchallengeable right to run any of their adherents for any post in the party as part of their campaign to win a majority, it is possible that they will win and as a result institute *their* regime in the party. The comrades of the Majority will be the first to defend them in this right, for upon the free exercise of this right depends the successful maintenance of democracy within the Fourth International. Moreover both the Majority and the Minority have agreed to eliminate all question of split, expulsions, or resignations. This means that if either the Majority or the Minority win the party, those in opposition who lost have agreed to abide by the incoming regime and to work loyally in accordance with the principles of centralism. Hence every serious member of the party must ask himself and the Minority caucus: will it be the political line of the *Defeatists*, the line of the *Doubtists*, or the line of those Minority comrades who agree politically with the Majority?

Our movement has been built through great sacrifices. Hundreds upon hundreds, and not only in the Soviet Union, have given their lives for the basic line of the Fourth International. That line was forged through costly experiences and struggles both organizational and political. It must not be given up lightly, for administrative reasons, for emotional reasons, or because of temporary and passing moods. The reasoning of those older experienced proletarian comrades who hammered out the Fourth International in collaboration with the heroic few who first took up the fight against Stalinism as part of world reaction in 1923–24 must not be rejected lightly. The coming period is not just one of reaction and terror but one filled

* Freud was fond of pointing out in his works that the victims of even such constant occurrences of everyday life as *forgetting*, for example, are never conscious of the cause and are indeed the stoutest deniers of the real cause, and that only by the most vigorous discipline and searching analysis can the victim become aware of the true cause.

with the brightest vistas for our movement. The proletariat took one–sixth of the globe in the last war. In this one they will smash the bloody rule of capitalism forever. But if we are to succeed it can be only with the line of the Fourth International—a hard basic principled political line that is not easily changed or traded for a mess of organizational pottage.

DECEMBER 1, 1939.

P.S.: Since writing the above, I have been informed that Abern is running for City Organizer in New York with excellent chances for success. What does this mean? Will Abern break from the political hegemony of the Defeatists and Doubtists on whose organizational strength he is riding and carry out the political line of the Majority? Or is he merely the organizational blackjack with which the Defeatists and Doubtists intend to slug their way into political power? The fact that the Minority is ousting such a competent Bolshevik organizer as Bert Cochran should open the eyes of many to the fact that there is something more serious than just the organizational or administrative question at stake in this struggle.

THE ABERN CLIQUE

By Joseph Hansen

The issues in dispute over politics, sociology, and philosophy in the factional struggle are now absolutely clear. The Majority has established that the opposition is colored by the alien bourgeois philosophy of Burnham, that it has suppressed its principled differences over the class analysis of the Soviet Union for the sake of a bloc against the proletarian wing of the party, that it is shifting more and more to outright defeatism in the Soviet Union in the event of imperialist attack. The Majority has established that it, contrary to the opposition, supports and defends dialectical materialism and uses the dialectic method in its analyses, that the Soviet Union is unmistakably a degenerated workers' state and therefore must be defended by the world proletariat in any struggle between it and a capitalist state, and that its analyses of the events in Poland and Finland which have been in dispute have been far more correct than those of the opposition. As for the political tendency and social roots of the opposition, the Majority has established that they are predominantly petty-bourgeois.

In my article written some four months ago, "Organizational Methods and Political Principles," I attempted to make clear for opposition comrades new to the party that Bolsheviks upon determining in any struggle what principles are involved take sides according to their position upon those principles and not according to secondary questions such as the so-called "organization" or "regime" question posed in this struggle by the opposition. I then described some of the methods of the Abern clique in past struggles, and showed that these methods are unprincipled and opposed to Bolshevik methods. I intimated that the Abern clique had not been dissolved at the time of entry into the Socialist Party and that it was participating as an unprincipled group in the present struggle, with Burnham as its brain trust and Shachtman as its attorney.

Although I was not the only one to call attention to this fact, Comrade Trotsky himself pointing out that "Abern and only he, has his own traditional group" to which all "others who hold various reasons for criticism and discontent cling" and that on the basis of his own "personal and immediate observations during the past three years" he could assert "that the Abern faction has existed uninterruptedly, statically if not 'dynamically,'" the leaders of the opposition chose to maintain that there was no such thing as an Abern group.

"Cannon knows how spurious it is to inject into the present dispute the 'Abern question.' He knows what every informed party leader, and many members, know, namely, that for the past several years at least there has been no such thing as an 'Abern group.'" (Shachtman in *Internal Bulletin,* Vol. II, No. 7, P. 18).

Abern himself in a letter to Trotsky dated February 6, 1940, and distributed in mimeograph form by the opposition declares: "Your comment about a 'Communist Party group which Abern carried over into the Communist League of America' is sheer fiction. Since our entry into the Socialist Party—years ago—there has been only one permanent faction in the Party—Cannon's. From the moment of the Fourth Internationalists' entry into the Socialist Party, and also during the entire existence of the Socialist Workers Party, there has existed no group separate and apart in the Party—except the Cannon clique. The so-called Abern faction is a Cannon phantasy."

On top of this there is the opposition document entitled "On Organizational Methods" dated March 7, 1940, and signed by the "POLITICAL COMMITTEE MINORITY." Here are some of the more flagrant bits which strike the eye in this little masterpiece of falsehood:

"The opening gun fired *publicly* in the party on 'Abernism' was the article on 'Organizational Methods and Political Principles,' written by an expert on both questions, Comrade Jos. Hansen, who repeats in somewhat modified form the gossip and old wives' tales with which his faction has kept the party corridors alive in the past half year. . . . It would be impossible to write a document of some 7,000 words, as Hansen does, without including in it some facts. But in no document, at least in our present dispute, has any comrade succeeded in reducing the number of facts to such a rigid minimum as Hansen . . . read through the whole article and note that nowhere in his polemic does he bother himself with a quotation from a single document; nowhere does he bother himself with propping his extravagant assertions against the opposition with a single fact . . . It is more basically to be explained by the fact that there are not enough facts to go around for proving all his assertions or even one-tenth of them . . . Hansen's polemical style is the 'bridge' where he meets such old hands at the game as Yaroslavsky and Harry Gannes . . . The fact is that Cannon, like every other leading comrade in the party, knew perfectly well that the old Weber-Muste-Abern group had been dissolved and no longer existed. . . ."

After these quotations, I think I may be permitted to conclude with all fairness to the opposition leaders that they claim the Abern clique was dissolved at the time of the entry into the Socialist Party, that it was never resurrected, and that any reference to such a clique by the Majority—including Comrade Trotsky—brands them as falsifiers, Yaroslavskys and Harry Gannes. There is no evidence, no facts, the Abern clique is nothing but a "Cannon phantasy."

Whom are we to believe?

In the Spring of 1936 the Cannon-Shachtman entry faction of the Workers Party won a decisive majority at the convention and the Trotskyists entered the Socialist Party. The entry and non-entry factions were officially dissolved and the rank and file prepared for united work within the Socialist Party. But so far as the Abern clique was concerned it went out of existence only on the official record. In reality the Abern clique continued a subterranean existence. I shall prove this to the hilt with fact after fact as demanded of me by the opposition leaders including Abern. I shall use as the source of my facts the mountainous correspondence of this clique in which I engaged as a full-fledged member in direct violation, with the other members, of the Marxist precept that unprincipled factions have no justification for existence in the party of the proletariat.

From this correspondence I shall prove not only the fact of the clique's existence, but its unprincipled character, its anti-Bolshevik methods, its damage to our party. I shall prove that following the entry into the Socialist Party, the Abern clique continued uninterruptedly its basic line of undermining and attacking alleged Cannonites, of building up and lauding genuine Abernites. Let me emphasize this point, *the facts I cite cover the period following the entry convention after the factions were "liquidated."* It covers precisely the period for which the opposition leaders have demanded *facts.*

This correspondence reveals at the same time that Cannon, far from dominating the Political Committee was frequently in a minority, that there were serious differences between him on the one hand and Burnham-Shachtman on the other upon more than one occasion, and that Abern was always keenly interested in these differences and quick to capitalize upon them in a factional manner.

Let us proceed with the "empiric" evidence demanded of me by Shachtman, Burnham, and . . . Abern.

A letter from Abern dated July 26, 1936:

> "I have received your letter of July 20 and also airmailed papers with note enclosed on latest situation.
>
> "Enclosed are three items which I want *returned* to me right away, after reading:
>
> "a. Report on Chicago YPSL convention. Is only copy and I shall require.
>
> "b. On problems and a situation in China from our comrade. (Graves is the comrade. A member of the present opposition.—JH) Short on copies, too hard to get more made.
>
> "c. Ciliga: same as 'b.'
>
> "So upon reading, return at once, so I can use for others, instead of destroying this

time at your end. Been so much of late to do technically that one has to curtail as much as possible."

The rest of the letter is an analysis of the Maritime situation with suggestions as to the line that should be followed. (Barney Mayes and I were editing the Voice of the Federation in San Francisco). Note the "return at once," the reference to "others," the "instead of destroying this time at your end." The clique was held together by circulating confidential documents concerning the Political Committee, etc. These documents were generally either destroyed or returned. I referred to this practice in my previous article under the heading, "'Inside Dope'—the Underground Organizational Method."

II.

A letter from Abern dated August 29, 1936:

"I have been greatly occupied in the recent period with many meetings and other activities, so that it has not been possible to write as fully as I might. However, others undertook to write to you fellows to give you some idea of the activities and problems before us. And on the exceptional matter of AJ's philosophical and, hence, political, shift of position, Natie [Gould—JH] will write to you, until I can get round to those and other matters myself. For the next days, yet, it looks as if I'll continue to have to meet a good deal at committee, party gatherings, etc. I mention these things so that you will have no misgivings.

"As a matter of fact developments in many ways have been very good indeed, from our standpoint, and it made me and other comrades more sanguine or hopeful than they have ever been in a long, long time. The work of our comrades in Chicago, in Akron, out your way and other places has been having its effects and one could easily observe a definitely changing attitude toward us. Basic political perspectives have tended to be adopted along our outlook, etc. And so on. The sudden loss of AJ to our movement of course is a loss for all; we, naturally, had most to expect of that association. But his decision is irrevocable, and after having today read his elaborated statement on his present philosophic outlook, there is nothing for us to do but to accept the fact, gird our loins, so to speak, and press onward as before. But I am not dilating on this matter before, and meanwhile Natie will send you a bit more information. Interim, too, until the Club sends an official statement to the comrades throughout the country, the information conveyed to you is confidential, for yourself, Barney, Ruth."

In my previous article I mentioned this organizational method of notifying us of decisions or statements of the Political Committee prior to their appearance through official party channels. In this case Abern had to prepare his ranks for a severe shock. A.J. Muste, co-leader with him of the faction, had just gone back to God. This made a profound impression throughout the party, and especially among those who had considered him a leader. I almost broke with the clique then and there, but I was still poisoned against the Bolshevik wing of the party and had not yet seen its leaders in action at close range.

Note Abern's remark regarding Muste's defection: "AJ's philosophical and, hence, political, shift." In his present bloc with Burnham, Abern is demanding along with Shachtman, "since when" were philosophical positions connected "directly" or "immediately" with political positions? "Abern long ago came to the conclusion that Marxism is a doctrine to be honored but a good oppositional combination is something far more substantial." (Trotsky in Internal Bulletin, Vol. II. No. 9, p. 13).

Another paragraph of this letter which reveals Abern's methods suggests that Maurice Spector go to the coast for work on the Voice but adds that "in view of the official request made on the matter, not to have any false hopes at your end." That is, it would be blocked by Cannon. Spector, as mentioned in my previous article, was the "Lenin of America" who came down from Canada to save us from the entry.

The letter ends with a request to send copies of the Voice to John Poulos, Nathan Gould, Lyman Paine, and McKinney. (All in the present opposition.)

III.

A letter from N. Gould, not dated.

> "Dear Comrade Hansen—
>
> "I sent this brief statement of the A.J. defection to you a few days ago but it was returned for lack of a proper address—I will follow this up with more details and more information. Please destroy the enclosed.
>
> *"N. Gould."*

Short and to the point. Formally Gould had adjured his former factionalism and was engaged in loyally cooperating to remove factional hangovers. When Gould, today in the petty-bourgeois opposition, speaks about the better preparedness of the youth for underground work in the coming period one cannot help smiling ironically. Gould should know.

IV.

A letter from R. Ferguson [a member of the present opposition] of Akron, dated Aug. 28, 1936:

> "The other comrades in Akron [Note "the other comrades"—JH] have been informed of the Muste defection, and once having gotten over the shock of it, will be able to take it in their stride, I believe. In fact, I believe that we comrades who are engaged in day to day activity in unions, etc. especially will have little time for despair about this matter. There is no use denying, however, that the ramifications will be great . . . By way of 'consolation' [!] one can be aware of the fact that it's better this happened (if it had to happen) while we're more or less buried in the SP, while no faction fight is going on, and that Muste's break is a definitive one (one that he will not be able to attract any following to). Things in NYC are moving ahead—in our direction, even better than expected. In our locality, Cleveland, Yougstown, Muste defection is creating hardly a ripple. Better wait for official news from center before broaching Muste case to other comrades except. . . ."

It is clear from this that our task was not to drive home the meaning of this defection of Muste, that it was a result of a philosophical difference with Marxism and that his political position in the previous faction struggle had flowed from his philosophical views—but rather to cover up this defection, and to minimize it, to obscure it and to ward off the repercussions it would have in the ranks of the clique. Abern is repeating this same tactic now in the case of Burnham's attacks against dialectical materialism. The parallel between Abern's obscuring the meaning of Muste's defection and his present covering up of the meaning of Burnham's views is so striking that it cannot escape the attention of anyone acquainted with the entry struggle and the present struggle.

Ferguson enclosed a carbon copy of a letter of his to Max Sterling then making a tour of the revolution in Spain. This letter, dated August 20, 1936, reports of a conference of Abernites. Here are some significant paragraphs:

> "A.J. returned day before yesterday, and we are having a conference beginning this afternoon. Coincidentally, Wilson [B.J. Widick—JH] and I (possibly Lear) are here from Akron, and also Natie. Reports and discussion of perspectives will be the order of the day.
>
> "Natie and I had a long talk with Marty [Abern—JH] on the situation in various parts of the country, which I will proceed to retail to you now. Other events happening in the last few days in NYC will try to find a place also, later. Natie will be writing to you next week probably, so he'll give information here omitted."

The report from Ferguson to Sterling proceeds with an analysis of clique activities from coast to coast, particularly in critical trade union situations.

> "In connection with this whole Coast matter the attitude of C. etc. [Cannon-Shachtman—JH] has been despicable—pooh-poohing the whole thing, refusing to take it seriously, issuing no directives, even refusing to take up the problem without an 'official' report instead of thru the information Marty receives. Marty has been spending an enormous amount of time giving good advice, as the whole task has

> devolved upon himself. . . . One new problem is getting someone to take over Barney's editorship so that he will be able to devote his time to getting around the Coast waterfront amongst the workers, etc. Maurice has been considered for this work, but declines."

Barney Mayes was at this time temporary editor of the Voice and the problem was to find someone within the clique less vulnerable to attack to replace him. Naturally the party view on the matter was something that entered into the clique calculations but only as a nuisance that could not conveniently be over-looked. As a matter of fact the clique operated in the maritime situation pretty much as an autonomous group. Barney solved the situation by taking the post himself.

> "In Minneapolis, local 574 has merged with local 544 (AFL paper outfit) on a basis which we consider was not necessary as it involved making too many concessions. There were only about 50 members of the AFL union, but representation on the new executive board will be 3-3, with an 'impartial' chairman, who happens to be a Tobin man. We do not yet have complete information on all that took place during the negotiations, but Jim is supposed to have been there for 5 weeks, and is still not back in NYC. . . . In Minneapolis, the SP is supposed to number 150; the former WP having about 80 comrades. The SP is running only one candidate in opposition to the F-L Party in Minnesota, in spite of the fact that the F-L P is supporting Roosevelt. Our comrades are supposed to be in a position to control the state SP."

It is clear from this that the "problem" of Minneapolis did not arise the day Shachtman in the present struggle reported his failure to storm its proletarian barriers.

> "In Boston the remnants of the old faction struggle still remain in a sharp form, due of course to the JGW [John G. Wright—JH] influence. Shachtman's report is newsed about in a factional manner, while the report has not yet been given to the club. Practically all work is sabotaged as a result. To this has also been added the irresponsible methods of Konikow who gets himself elected to the SEC of the SP without consulting anyone. Needless to say, consultation would have doubtless defeated this move, for this person. Fortunately, Boston is the worst place for this sort of thing."

The Abern clique had not yet uncovered an attorney to name JGW the "red professor" and the "major Yaroslavsky" but the line is the same.

> "In Chicago, our comrades in the YPSL particularly, and also in the SP, have been making more progress than anywhere else in the country. Natie will doubtless write you as to the details there. They have defeated several anti-Trotskyist resolutions in the SP there so far—one that no one could attack the 2nd International. They are successfully solidarizing themselves with the ranks, accepting posts, etc. on the basis of their political issues and not—a la Cannon—by keeping their mouths shut on political issues. They also defeated a motion calling for the abolition of the *Soc. Appeal.*"

This report on Chicago which at that time was an Abernite stronghold is another of the Abern methods—lauding the clique members and constantly spotlighting them as if the party revolved about them and their importance.

> "Finally, in New York, up until just the last week one could speak of the work in the SP and YPSL proceeding at a snail's pace, according to the Cannonian precept of proceeding 'without discussion' and grabbing off posts quietly, etc. However, for a number of reasons, this situation is now taking a turn for the better. This can be attributed to the following reasons: (1) press of international events, Spain, France, and Russia; (2) probably Max [Shachtman—JH] learned from LD in clearer fashion that at all costs we must press forward on these questions; (3) Cannon's being out of town, whereby those of his followers remaining are more readily influenced by the pressure of revolutionary events abroad,

as well as by the pressure of the former Cannon caucus's rank and file, many comrades of which are openly grumbling about the course being followed. In this connection we hear remarks from these comrades, such as, 'If we had it to do over again, we'd vote with you,' and 'We were bull-shitted out of the NM." [New Militant—JH] (this from Max!) At the club meeting a week ago Monday West [Burnham—JH] proposed for the first time a discussion on perspectives in the SP. The discussion was encouraging from our point of view, as it brought out that the former Cannonites are shifting their views more in the direction of ours under pressure of forces I outlined above."

Note the Abern line in the above paragraph that Cannon does not respond to events in contrast to the dynamic Abernite ability to meet events well in advance. It is because of their inability to graduate from this thesis that the Abernites require the "inside dope." It is their way of keeping at the head end of events rather than the tail end.

The report to Sterling lists the club [Political Committee] maneuvers and negotiations with Tyler and Zam, and then goes into the question of Muste's defection which is explained as follows (again note the parallel between Muste in that fight and Burnham in the present one):

"For this there are a number of explanations, none of them valid by themselves. In my opinion the trip abroad, [Muste visited Trotsky in Norway—JH] which he took to 'think things over' brought him in contact at first hand with the huge armies of capitalism: and he grasped with his senses what from this distance he had only been able to envisage intellectually before. As against these military establishments and the apparent hold their masters had over the masses, he could for the first time (at the conference for the 4th International) appreciate the weakness of our forces. Feeling unable to cope with the tasks of the future, he reverted to the ideas of his youth, which he held during the last war.

"A factor which, though lying in the background, is probably of the greatest importance is the terrific battering he took in the factional struggle of the past two years. The trip abroad gave him his first real opportunity to take stock of his past in the light of aims he had set for himself in his youth. He doubtless saw himself now associated with people like his former faction opponents, in whom he could place no confidence and whose ethics in the movement are repugnant to any sensitive person. In fact, in his private conversations in NYC he stressed a great deal the matter of ethics and morals in the movement, stating his opposition to the theory of 'anything goes'. Of course, he intertwines this matter of ethics with his Christian pacifism, and attributes bureaucracy, etc. to the fact that the movement believes in and uses violence!!!"

We too are amused at Muste's beliefs and yet Abern now finds it possible to make another bloc with a man like Burnham whose religion differs from Muste's only in its being less prayerful.

"Will have to be drawing this letter to a close, so you will get it before sailing. There are of course a great number of things to be said about every situation I've touched on. Just a few concluding remarks. The effects of the Muste defection will of course practically be to wipe out the influence of the former Muste-Abern* group; discredit our past struggle, make it more difficult for us to get a hearing in the future. It would also be expecting too much to think that factional advantage will not be taken of the matter. The effect on our own ranks so far has been one of deep shock, but I think that we need not fear demoralization except in perhaps isolated instances. Time alone can tell on this. As for myself, as well as to others, it is the international aspect that is the most disturbing, for

* The leaders of the Minority on the Political Committee accuse me of committing a "petty falsification" in calling the anti-entrists the "Muste-Abern group." However, as can be seen in this report circulated in the Abern clique after it became a "Cannon phantasy" as Abern puts it so tellingly, this was the ordinary label. The group really had different names at different times according to whoever happened to lend his prestige and attorneyship to the clique.

over there where there is so little time left this blow will be felt most keenly. I do not think I need dilate on this. It can also be left to the imagination just what attention will be paid to our tendency in the US by comrades abroad for some time to come.

"In the face of these problems, old and new, a number of us conversing together in NYC on several occasions drew some rather far-reaching conclusions. The most important of these was: the old leadership is done for; together we must work to educate ourselves and others, with the conscious aim of developing a new cadre of leaders. In doing this we look primarily to the youth. Every single one of us is agreed on this perspective. As for the perspective in the SP, as I've already noted, the Cannonites are coming more and more towards our position in the last few weeks, and under the pressure of revolutionary events, in the future it is not excluded that splits may further develop in their camp."

This report it must again be noted was written *after* the entry, *after* the factions were dissolved, *after* the Abern group was officially no more. It was sent overseas to Max Sterling then in Spain. That its discovery by any of the countless enemies of the Fourth International could have proved most damaging and crippling to our work in the Socialist Party was of far less concern to the clique than keeping secret our own existence as a group separate and apart from the rest of the party.

V.

A report, "The Situation in Akron, Ohio," dated Oct. 4, 1936, was circulated at this time in the clique. Pencilled on top of this report are the significant words: "Return or destroy." The discovery of this report by the wrong people likewise could have dealt a stiff blow to our work in the Socialist Party.

Muste's defection had shaken me deeply. During this period I was lax in returning or destroying documents and hence still possess it. This particular document has little political interest at the present time. It is typical of the countless reports circulated in the clique. It gives the "inside dope" on Ohio and what the boys are doing there.

VI.

A letter from Abern dated October 18, 1936:

> "Enclosed, too, is a copy of latest issue of POUM paper. Please let me hear if you get copies direct from Barcelona. Max Sterling told me that he had had your name placed there on the mailing list,—your Salt Lake City address. Probably the paper is arriving there. You might arrange to have it forwarded. By now you should have gotton back from Barney the various items you've let him have hitherto."

I never did get the POUM paper but at this late date I nevertheless thank Sterling for his kind thoughts for another member of the clique while he was touring Spain. As to the "various items," Abern always worried about those as will be seen in later quotations. Rightly so, these "items" concerned the most confidential occurrences within the Political Committee, occurrences which no one had any business taking out of that Committee, and especially passing on through the circles of an irresponsible clique which might contain in its ranks a stool pigeon such as a Right Wing stooge of the SP, a Lovestoneite, a Thomasite, even a provocateur or—it is by no means excluded—an agent of the GPU. Looking back over this period it seems incredible that the whole Trotskyite strategy in the Socialist Party was not exploded a dozen times over. Who can vouch that information did not leak into the enemy camps? Certainly not Abern.

VII.

A letter from Abern dated October 24, 1936:

> "I had expected to hear from you before now, if only briefly, in reply to my letter, etc. of a few weeks ago. But possibly, and I surely hope not, you have been ill; or you have been too busy to write; or you have decided to discontinue writing, which is your right. Still, I rather expected an acknowledgement, anyway, of receipt of communications . . . I should like to know, for one, if Comrade Cannon got the letter to him that I sent through you. Also, I have been awaiting the return of the items

I sent you on occasions in the past weeks. I believe I suggested that you regard my recent letters for yourself only, since Barney, I have presumed, did not require further such information or aid as I rendered, or tried to, in the past.

"Did Barney return the letters he had of you, or did he by any chance lose or misplace them; or did he, though I assume otherwise, give them inadvertently to any persons he shouldn't? I should like to know about these things and, of course even more important, how the maritime set-up looks today; so oblige me even if only with a brief response now."

The second paragraph in the letter above indicates that Abern was worried over relations between Cannon and Barney and the possibility that Barney had shown him correspondence which would have proved Abernism far from being a "dead dog."

At this time I was beginning to realize the implications of Muste's role in the movement; for the first time I had met Cannon then in California and discovered that he had neither horns nor hoofs nor forked tail; that he was a cold, grim politician; a person who lived on the same poverty-stricken scale as the rest of us, a leader who took part in branch activity—Cannon molasses for Abernite flies, naturally, but still the clique descriptions of him were disappointingly not quite accurate or else I had within me a touch of the rottenness that tended one toward Cannonism. At the same time, Barney told me emphatically that he was breaking off all relations with Abern, advised me to do likewise, informed me that Cannon was the only real Bolshevik in the American movement and its real leader and real expounder of Trotsky's views; and that in Barney's estimation Abern was an incorrigible intriguer and the "Stalin of America."

I was rather taken aback at Barney's inexplicable reversal in position as up to that minute Barney had been the real Abern representative on the West Coast. But Barney's sudden switch did not sway me. It seemed completely unmotivated, unexplainable, especially in view of his previous venomous stories about Cannon in the Communist Party days. I considered it a capitulation by Barney, a move on his part to curry favor. I did not even inquire of Cannon his views on Barney and Barney's politics. I can truthfully say that I was never more suspicious of any man than I was of Cannon—and this suspicion was wholly the result of Abernism.

VIII.

A letter from Abern dated November 2, 1936:

> "What I said in my letter to Barney was that I *hoped* that the club would now seriously begin to take up problems of the Coast. Further than that I would not at present say. I do not know if the Center has written even to Barney. You would probably know. Nevertheless, it will be seen in not too great a time, I trust, if hopes are real. Cannon's presence on the Coast should certainly help.
>
> "Of course I am glad to continue a *personal* correspondence with you. I wanted to give you the opportunity, if you thought it unnecessary now or were too busy, to give up such correspondence without any hesitation for any reason on your part. But I would ask that such exchange of letters, etc. be strictly limited to ourselves, not to be shown to others. OK?"

In view of the fact that the leaders of the opposition including Abern himself have hurled the lie in my face regarding the rather mild statements I made in my previous article, I feel politically justified in violating this request of Abern's at the present time.

The letter continues with criticism—to me a rank and filer—of certain actions of the Political Committee:

> "A few weeks ago the club made a decision to liquidate our printing plant altogether. Perhaps you have heard of this by now. Since the plant is no more, there isn't much use going into the details now. I thought the decision was a terribly wrong one and I opposed the step strongly. Likewise Swabeck was opposed to the liquidation. I saw no need for this step since in my opinion this action will make much harder the carrying through of our publication program and particularly, I think, will effect the Ap-

peal's future. Costs will be strongly increased. It was hard going for the plant in this period, as was to be expected while we were in the SP. Nevertheless the plant, I think, could have been maintained, additional work obtained, management efficiency improved and more regular issuance of our works assured. Others thought that in this period we could go along without the plant and in the future raise the funds for another printing plant. Well, if funds could be obtained in the *future* for a new plant, it seems reasonable to me they could be gotten now to maintain and improve the plant *today*. And I offered, if assured that every effort would then be made to continue the plant right along, to try to obtain the needed few hundred dollars. I think the club tried to make an objective decision all right; but I think it made a damned bad one in all respects. If you are interested to know a bit more, other than the above statement of fact, on this matter and its significance, let me know.

"Have to look around to see what is what, so will close at this point. I hope certainly to hear regularly from you and again request that the correspondence be limited strictly between us two."

If anyone is still puzzled as to why the question of the press suddenly became a hot issue at this time among the Trotskyists in the Socialist Party, he now has the full explanation.

As to the merits of the controversy, naturally we could not make inquiries of Cannon even if we had been inclined to such action, since that would have exposed the existence of our clique. Abern enjoyed the advantage that a clique always enjoys and which cements it together, he circulated the inside dope and he circulated just his version of it.

IX.

A letter from Abern dated November 9, 1936:

> "The enclosed item is *only* for *your* information and indicates that in the next months we should know pretty much where everything stands in the S.P. With the elimination of the openly Right Wing elements in the S.P. in the past months and with the likelihood that additional kindred elements can be perhaps pushed out, the S.P. physically will be considerably changed. We will be able to contend more directly with the bulk of variety of centrist elements. It is indeed a not very large S.P. now to be observed. Probably the Farmer-Labor issue will be the one which will show us how far, or otherwise, we can get with what calls itself the 'Militant' tendency. Tonight we hold our first joint meeting with the 'Militants,' at which I imagine there will be mainly reports and little discussion—sort of laying the ground and sounding out the situation. . . . Please *return quickly* to me the enclosed item."

The letter mentions that Harry Milton, another member of the clique, (A member of the present opposition.) is coming to the West Coast to live and that it would be good to look for work for him "as a seaman or otherwise." Milton went to Spain instead.

I overlooked "returning quickly" the "enclosed item." In fact I have not returned it yet. It is dated November 5, 1936, and is a copy of a letter from "Marty" to "Al" (Abern to Glotzer, who is also a member of the present opposition.)

Besides all the inside dope on what is happening on the Political Committee and in the negotiations and maneuvers in the S.P. the "enclosed item" includes the following interesting point:

> "8. —In view of the unquestioned weakness and failures of proper correspondence from the center with some rationalizing explanations thereof, again it was decided that it is now politically necessary to develop the correspondence to and from our center to our comrades. We shall see what comes of it."

There were no weaknesses or failures of "proper" correspondence among the members of the nonexistent Abern clique! The unreturned "item" concludes:

> "Also I think it is now necessary to begin to examine our past period in the S.P. We have been satisfied until now with being permitted our democratic rights to espouse our ideas

while at the same time carrying through whatever decisions of the Party were adopted on basic principles. We can only do this for a given period and then decide whether we can still fruitfully carry on in that manner, or whether our break with centrism is to be at a given time both organizational as well as political. In brief, how long can we remain together with centrists and reformists in the same organization. I think we are approaching the time when these questions will have to be settled. I hope for a healthy, positive settlement with all concurring but we shall have to wait to see, more anon."

Many of us were beginning to examine the past period in the S.P., and also the question of the validity of the entry. Abern however was not interested in reevaluating his position on the entry. It will become clear in the quotations I shall cite presently that day by day he grew less and less interested in this question. The above letter shows that Abern is apparently beginning to move for stepping up the tempo in the S.P.—the perspective of quick departure—again without opportunity for the Political Committee views to be debated or expressed or even its knowledge that its decisions and perspectives were being questioned by an organized underground clique. This is Abern's idea of democratic centralism. Democracy for himself and his clique at all times and in all places. The centralism is something for lip service.

X.

A letter from Abern dated November 20, 1936:

> "There have been a good many specific or concrete developments in N.Y.C, all of which will, I believe, tend more quickly to unify our efforts on a national scale. But I assume that through regular channels, that is, your fraction, you are being kept adequately informed on all the important happenings, and so I won't go into them here. In Chicago, too, matters have been working themselves out nicely. Natie Gould has been acting as secretary of the YPSL.
>
> "I believe you still have one item I sent you a while back, as of Nov. 5th."

As I remarked in my previous article, Abern has unquestioned administrative ability. He never missed an "item" that was supposed to be returned to the clique center.

XI.

A letter from Abern dated December 4, 1936:

> "Jack Wilson [B.J. Widick, another member of the present opposition.—JH] was in New York for a few days last week and returned to Akron the other day. That explains why recent requests to him could not be answered at once since the mail naturally reached him later. But what I wanted to say was that Jack had an opportunity to observe and to talk over developments with the comrades. He'll write to you adequately on all the important developments and therefore I'll refrain here except from some passing comments."

The letter continues with details about the organization of the mass meeting for the defense of Trotsky, news about developments in the S.P. in New York, and then adds:

> "Right now I am most concerned that the Socialist Appeal come out as a semi-monthly. That is, despite the notions of some comrades on the Coast, our main political, ideological, centralizing medium. The biggest mistake we could make is to let the Appeal rest as a monthly, for Labor Action nor any publication having mainly an agitational character can possibly fill that role. In this field, all other publications have to take second place to the need to increase frequency of issue of the Appeal. If education and organization are to take place properly, it will have to be done through dissemination of our principle positions in adequate form and that can best be accomplished through the Appeal, our only medium, besides books, for presenting our complete ideological outlook. After all, whatever elements there are to be won in the SP—and I don't think they are many—have to be won to a fundamental outlook, so that with any organizational eventuality in the SP, they will stay with us and not horse around

unable to make up their minds where they want to be. But, I forget, I am leaving it to Jack to write to you rather fully on happenings. I may say in passing, until I get a chance to write more fully, that the center's line in the recent months has been fundamentally correct, as against the conceptions put forward by others here and there. Of course, carrying thru that line in practice is dependent upon persons and hence is not always as complete as one would like; but essentially the effort is being seriously made. It is foolish at this time to say just how it will all come out in the wash on a national scale, when we begin to figure up what we gave and what we got in return, but interim, make the most of it."

The California state Socialist Party had established Labor Action as its *official* weekly paper. It was an 8 column 4 page paper and hence, in conjunction with the Socialist Appeal then appearing monthly in magazine form, adequate for our needs at the time. Cannon was made the editor of Labor Action and hence we controlled its policy despite constant sideswipes from the Symes-Clement group. In view of its official status and the support given it by the Socialist Party and the freedom with which we could distribute it, Labor Action was of great importance to us. Abern, however, did not agree. This whole paragraph is an attack against Cannon. Its veiled nature is explained by the fact that I was wholeheartedly for Labor Action. Abern had to go easy while he straightened me out.

Another paragraph concerning a member of the clique who is with the present opposition[1] is of interest:

> "Before I forget: Frank G. of China has in mind to come to the U.S. again, this time to locate permanently, about February or March. The date is yet tentative. He inquires of the possibility, on his way from China, to earn bread and room if he should stop a little while in Frisco (I had suggested it previously). He is an accomplished journalist and editor in all respects; high political quality, as you've probably noted from his articles in the past ('Lucifer.') He'd make an excellent editor for a publication of ours. I imagine that he could easily be made use of in Frisco. My own opinion is that he ought to locate in some place in Chicago permanently, but that's up to him. But if he comes to Frisco for a while, (he'll probably head Eastward, though, since his wife is a Chicagoan they might decide to stay there), make use of him. Let me hear what prospects would be by way of work. Am dropping Cannon a note on this, but there's no need to mention the matter to him at all. Possibly Frank may change his mind and decide to stay still longer in China; he's been there now for many years."

The description of G. is typical of the descriptions that circulated in the clique. Whether they deserved it or not—rank and filers such as I had no way of judging or knowing—the members were without exception dynamic, independent, gifted, sensitive to events, and of high political caliber, always raising all discussions to a higher political level. The descriptions of members of the party outside our clique naturally were as venomous as those were laudatory. I wrote not a few deprecatory descriptions myself which got into wrong hands as some of the comrades may recall, especially prior to the entry. In this same letter, Abern "dilates" with a few high words of praise for Gould's work in Chicago.

I note that on the last page of this letter Abern got his carbon in the typewriter backward so that it typed upon the back of the letter instead of making a carbon copy. This was an administrative error seldom made by Abern. However he can check everything except the last paragraph cited above in the carbon copies of this correspondence which he no doubt still keeps in his files for the sake of posterity.

XII.

A letter from Widick dated "Wednesday" but which internal evidence places at about this time:

> "The inclosed letter will give you some of the inside dope on the auto strike. The gods of fortune were smiling on me when they saw fit to

1. My impression, drawn from Abern's correspondence, that Frank G. was a member of the clique was mistaken. The error was cleared up later in the factional struggle.—JH (1972).

have me in Flint just before the battle. It makes the CP attack here futile during this period.

"In view of the new attacks in the Daily W. (Tuesday edition and very much worthwhile having) it looks like more will be tried here. I'm hurrying to build enough real support against both the CP and reactionaries so that the lone wolf can come through with flying colors. My chances are 60–40."

Apparently I returned the "inclosed letter" with the "inside dope" as I do not find it in my files. Widick's modesty should not be taken as an especially personal characteristic of his; it is one of the distinctive features of the entire clique. In these internal letters it sometimes becomes quite a strain to live up to each others' coups—a fantastic life of "lone wolf" deeds and always coming through "with flying colors" against odds that ranged from 60–40 to 1–100.

"My feeling toward the SP is like yours. We are engaged in major struggles and are trying to recruit on a Trotskyite basis. The SP can put nothing in our road so what the hell are a few months one way or the other."

It is apparent that Hansen's position on the entry is beginning to shift. Cannon's presence in California is shaking him loose from the pressure of Abern's underground revolutionary line.

XIII.

A letter from Widick dated "Sunday."

"Turning to the national situation, it was my good fortune to spend a weekend recently in New York. Frankly I went there in a highly critical state of mind especially in regard to how matters were proceeding in relation to our work in the SP. It was my tentative opinion that we were wasting time and energy in the SP and that we ought to pull out around convention time after utilizing the pre-convention discussion period to grab whatever was worthwhile in the SP."

Was our Political Committee worried at that time about manifestations of impatience and ultra-leftism in our ranks? This was due to the Abern clique and its "highly critical state of mind" about which it was quite frank in its intermember correspondence. But this "critical state of mind" could not be allowed by Abern to develop to the point of open manifestation. (There was no "front" for the clique and it was not to find a "front" until 1939).

"I have always felt that one of the chief weaknesses in the SP was the lack of an adequate press to present our views. Because of this I consider building up the Appeal as one of the major tasks before us. We cannot only win elements through our press but also determine where we stand, judging by the support given to it. Naturally, since our struggle is primarily an ideological one, a theoretical organ of the Appeal nature becomes our chief press weapon. Papers like Labor Action are a most valuable supplement, in my estimation, and incidentally, I haven't been receiving any copies although I placed a bundle order of ten per issue.

"I should add, in regard to the SP, that my NY trip convinced me that my tentative position was partly erroneous due primarily to my being away from the scene and thus not making proper judgement. I was surprised and pleased to see that on most major matters the leading comrades in the center viewed things eye to eye. The ranks seem to be picking up too and things are moving quite rapidly so that one can never tell exactly what will happen."

Formally the Abern group does not exist and in the center—Cannon is in California editing Labor Action—Abern, Shachtman, Burnham, Carter, Spector, etc. are seeing eye to eye. Nevertheless, "one can never tell exactly what will happen."

XIV.

A letter from Max Sterling (A member of the present opposition.) dated Dec. 25, 1936. After analyzing the situation, he begins straightening out Hansen on what is apparently a slight weakness in this comrade, a softness that if left uncounteracted might develop into full-blown conciliation to Cannonism:

"I want to say that I do not counterpose what is being done outside of NY with our problem here and it is for that reason that I believe that whatever opinions JPC may have in respect to what is to be done can very easily be reconciled with our own views here. For example, take Labor Action which I believe to be a very valuable weapon in the struggle for a revolutionary Socialist Party. Is there any reason why it should conflict with the Socialist Appeal which is more suitable as a theoretical expression for the left wing nationally while it must be admitted that Labor Action is more nearly a west coast weapon of an entirely different character, that is having a mass character? Each I believe can do yeoman work in its own sphere. The second point; what objections can one possibly have to the RSES which even at this early stage has achieved a certain separation between the left and right centrists? One has to admit that there is a special problem in New York that must be faced in a special way. Everything that is being done in the field is highly important and must naturally occupy our serious attention but is there any one who can reasonably say 'let us leave New York to its fate.' The thing that is objectionable in JCP's attitude is of course his presentation of his views as an ultimatum and his non-cooperative tone.

"Some time ago West, [Burnham—JH] in behalf of the Club, wrote a supposedly personal letter to JPC outlining the situation as he saw it in respect to the views held by the various members of the Club including JPC. For some reason he stated therein that there were four views in the Club regarding perspective in the SP. There was, of course, Cannon's view which he wrote was emphasis on the provinces and a head on collision in New York, there was his view which was not too much emphasis on NY but a long range perspective in the SP, there was Shachtman's view which was emphasis on New York plus a long range perspective in the SP and finally there was Abern's view of a head on collision and an early split from the SP. Now because I happen to know the facts especially as regards Abern's point of view I want to tell you that West's letter is absolutely wrong in this respect. Firstly I believe that aside from JCP's position there are amongst the Club members in NY hardly any differences of opinion and this includes Martin Abern. If there are any differences between West and Shachtman then they certainly haven't had a chance to come out as yet and as far as Abern is concerned the record in the club will show that Marty's position was essentially in line with the rest. How then is it that West can ascribe to Marty a point of view that he doesn't hold?

"I confess that the manner in which West wrote of what he thought was Marty's point of view despite the record is not very flattering to Marty. In short West based himself on a letter that Jack Wilson had written to Turner of Boston which the latter promptly turned over to the Club in which Jack did really express the view of a split perspective in the coming period, a conclusion which he had reached as a result of his local experience. And this view of Wilson's was immediately thought to have originated with Marty. Thus Wilson too is made out to be a dullard without an original thought in his head which is not flattering to him either. But the truth happens to be that before the discovery of this letter Marty and I too were sharply criticizing Jack for drawing conclusions that none of us, on the basis of our relatively short life in the SP, could possibly draw. Furthermore in the end Jack, on occasion of a visit to New York, was actually convinced of the correctness of Marty's point of view. The fact is that none of us, especially in view of the fluid situation in NY can say that it is time to say that we have exhausted the possibilities in the SP. One can go even further and say that with the SP as it is today with the old right wing on a national scale practically out, it is not at all impossible for us to gain the majority of what will remain in the SP. I can see from all this that when we said, upon deciding to go along with the majority into the SP we would not carry a factional attitude with us and what future struggles may arise on new issues and new alignments, that we kept our word and that we seek honestly without any factional lines to work with all who were our opponents in the past, yes and even to the extent of not harboring past reminiscences. I think this is true of all our former associates but having discussed this matter with Marty many times I can speak with certainty about ourselves. Therefore it irks us that any other opinion should get abroad as for example the impression that West has given out."

Officially we denied the existence of an Abern group and it irked us whenever our real existence was mentioned.

The irony of Sterling, a rank and filer like myself, discussing the confidential happenings in the Political Committee as if we constituted a high body of appeal, and in the same letter stating that "we kept our word" and that we went with the majority into the SP without carrying a "factional attitude" is I believe unconscious on Sterling's part. Sterling is really good-hearted. He has honest intentions; the only thing wrong is that his political development was arrested by Abern:

> "The mass meeting for the defense of LD held here last week was a tremendous success with close to 3000 persons in attendance and it hurt me to the heart when, as ticket-seller at the door, I had to stop selling tickets at 8:15 PM and I estimate that close to 2000 persons were turned away because of a full house. I will mention it to you Joe because it is not generally known but by a few of us that most of the credit should go to Marty who was in charge of all the preparations and organization of the meeting, and who worked for weeks, with that tireless energy and devotion to a task so characteristic of him, to put the meeting across. Shachtman was good enough after the meeting to tell Marty so in so many words. I don't want you to get the impression that I am a worshipper of Marty but I know his value to the movement and it is because I realize what a loss the movement will sustain if it loses Marty that I feel particularly keen about any attempts to kick him around as, unfortunately, has been done so many times in the past. It is unfortunately a weakness of Marty's to be unduly sensitive about such things but it seems to me that we should take this into account in the interests of the movement and to be able like Lenin to make good use of people. That is why I feel badly that Marty was not given due recognition for his work and was in fact not made a member of the Committee for the Defense of LD nor was he called upon to attend its meetings or to meet the various people who were on the committee as though he was an unwanted child who did only the dirty work. And not only here but in other respects is a similar attitude displayed by some members of the club even though the work of Marty since the entry has been irreproachable. I don't want to leave the impression that Marty and the others are not working together, the fact is that they are and especially is this true of Marty's relation to Shachtman but it is true nevertheless that if there are any old animosities it is certainly not Marty's fault. Still I suppose one can't leap over the past in a day and I sincerely hope that the future will show a vast improvement in the treatment of Marty as he really deserves to be."

The opposition speaks about a leader cult in our party. Re-read the above paragraph.

Sterling made the administrative error of getting the carbon backward on the last page of this letter, written after the clique no longer existed, however he can check back the other two pages which he no doubt has in his files to determine whether they were quoted correctly.

XV.

A letter from Abern dated December 25, 1936:

After going over the strike situation in San Francisco and the fight the Stalinists had waged successfully to oust us from the editorship of the Voice of the Federation, he goes into the internal situation:

> "Like yourself, we have all been very much occupied and have not had the opportunity to write very much to anyone. Jack Wilson promised to write to you—he was in NY some weeks ago—and give you a summary of events in the recent months. Possibly you

have heard from him by now. Max Sterling also promised to write to you this week-end on the more latter-day developments; and between the two you should be able to get a pretty good picture of affairs.

"I am enclosing a few items for your information. In some respects they are dated and events have confirmed them too. In reading them, keep in mind that it is comments to our own comrades so they may know how matters have transpired. As I have said before, I believe, the forward development has been very good in the recent period, as respects program and perspectives and I see no reason why this should not continue. A number of the irritations, etc. which I speak of, I have made an effort to clarify by discussions with the various comrades. In the Center we are now working more harmoniously than at any previous time, and I think that by and large we are all looking and deciding upon each question in an objective manner. Also, in respect to the Center's controversy with Cannon, I have been the one here who held definitely to the viewpoint that events, among other things, would make possible a solution and clarification of the *issues* involved, and have refused to exaggerate the differences in the issues, important as they were. Make no mistake about it, however, the differences were very important and if Cannon's line had been accepted, there would have been ruination for us in the S.P. I refer here to such questions as the formation of the New York RSES, the Appeal, national strategy, etc.—all of which are taken up elsewhere. But the Center stuck basically to its line and it has proved successful and profitable. Cannon evidently did what he pleased on the Coast, but luckily he was not able to affect matters in New York and nationally. Which is not to detract from the successes on the Coast in any way. Albeit, I see every reason why an effort should be made to come to a better understanding among all; and from what I know of the attitude of the comrades here (—after all, the Club are virtually all Cannonites and if they felt it necessary to disagree in the most extreme terms with JPC, you can bet there must have been damn good ground—) and the correspondence from the Coast, it is almost entirely up to C. There is not the slightest problem in this respect at this end. I have even urged that someone go to the Coast, in view of the possible effects on national policy, and endeavor to straighten out what I thought could be remedied. Now that Shachtman has to go to Mexico anyhow, in connection with LD matters, I again urged such a meeting and I think in some way this will be arranged. Observe that I have referred here to specific *issues* involved. As to the methods employed by Cannon that are involved, they deserve severe condemnation and could easily have proved ruinous to all, except that the Center observed great patience. When a Burnham, with the unanimous approval of all, can write a most sharp letter to C. charging him with the unhealthiest manifestations of Molinierism and all the other rotten phases in the French movement, you can guess how sharply wrought up the comrades here felt. But this aspect I leave aside here: let those who wish, learn. Suffice that I on my part did everything possible to indicate both the need and absolute likelihood to come to a healthy and satisfactory understanding between all concerned; if anything it was others who tended on occasion, perhaps for effect, to exaggerate this or that aspect . . . Another reason I urged that MS, [Max Shachtman—JH] for the Center, and JPC get together while MS is on his way, is that an understanding will make so much more fruitful the coming left wing conference in Chicago (not yet publicly made known). After all, we want to avoid having unnecessary struggles between us, and be, instead, in a position to go into the left wing conference with a positive program on all main questions."

I notice that in his document, "The Crisis in the American Party," Shachtman now declares: "It goes without saying that Cannon is not Molinier, and it would be useless to try to make me appear to say so." I am glad even at this late date to have this point cleared up, more or less officially. I was bothered about it when the charge was first made, even though only a rank and filer, and Cannon's complete silence upon the matter on the West Coast was something I did not dare break through. It would have exposed the underground clique. At the same time, the very fact that he did not discuss this charge with the rank and file and maintained strict silence about the differences in the leadership constituted such a striking contrast to Abern's sending me these confidential letters exchanged between the Political Committee members that it drove a little deeper the wedge that eventually broke me away from the Abern clique. I expected Cannon to appeal to the membership. That he did not was a strong lesson in the Bolshevik method of deciding issues and appealing to the membership only on principled grounds. I began wondering about the role of the leadership, its relationship with the rank and file, the *real* Bolshevik practice. I am still grateful to Cannon for his patience in answering all my questions at that time without knowing what motives were driving me to ask them.

> "Please regard all information sent you, enclosed material, etc. as *only personal information for yourself.* You can oblige me by reading same and then *returning* to me; thanks a lot."

The emphasis is in the original. The "enclosed material" was indeed of the most confidential nature and would have proved most damaging to the clique if it had been turned over to the Political Committee.

The letter mentions that "McKinney is in town for a few days and matters connected with the steel drive will be taken up. Bob Stiler also came in with him." Greetings are then given me from "Max, Rae, Milton, Weaver, et al" and the letter ends with a postscript:

> "P.S.—Will try to write again soon. Meanwhile, please favor me by acknowledging *receipt* of all this material *at once*; and please return quickly."

A typical communication in the non-existent Abern clique!

XVI.

At this time I left for a visit to Salt Lake City, believing that I had taken the "items" with me for reading at my leisure. On the bus I discovered that I had either lost them or left them in San Francisco. I immediately dropped a postcard to Abern informing him of this so that in case they were discovered and turned over to the Political Committee he would be prepared to brace himself.

Abern replied in a letter dated January 6, 1937:

> "I received your enclosed postcard from Salt Lake City. I am of course very much concerned about the letter and enclosures and hope everything will turn up all right. It is not necessary now to go into the adverse effects thereof, if otherwise. Is there any likelihood that anyone else would be visiting the chap you stayed with and thus perhaps pick up the items? Your belief that your friend is OK is a bit reassuring, but the main thing naturally is to find the stuff. Would it be advisable, in case you haven't done so, for you to drop a few words to your friend, telling him that you left some things behind and to be sure to put them carefully aside, etc. for you till your return? But this suggestion, if worthwhile, is probably pointless since this note, I presume, won't reach you till you are back in San Francisco. I hope your belief that you left the items behind and didn't lose same is the case. That seems likely, since the letter, etc. was pretty hefty and wouldn't easily fall out of your pocket, etc. without your noticing same.
>
> "I wish you would let me know at the first chance what's what, for I am disturbed about the matter. Perhaps—I hope so—this note will find you already back in San Francisco, and, too, with a job that you meanwhile located while on your trip.
>
> "Awaiting word that all is OK."

The friend with whom I stayed was O'Brien. He placed the "items" if I recall correctly in a drawer awaiting my return to San Francisco. I don't remember now whether as a reward I let him read them. I give him my permission to clear up this point with the leaders of the opposition of which he is now a member.

XVII.

A letter from Abern dated January 10, 1937:

> "Am awaiting word from you that everything is OK on the other matter. About Thursday–

Friday at the latest I am leaving New York for a few weeks and should like to hear from you by then. I'm assuming that you are now back in Frisco. When I know that you're definitely located again, I'll write to you on other matters. Meanwhile, admittedly, I am very desirous to learn about the other matter, for it is necessary to know what is what."

Abern was certainly worried about those "items." At this late date of course with Burnham's brains and Shachtman's tongue to defend him he can only smile at the fears and forebodings he harbored in those days that his clique would be exposed or brought prematurely to the surface.

XVIII.

A letter from Abern dated January 13, 1937:

> "I received today your letter of January 11 from Frisco and I am relieved to hear that everything is all right in respect to the material. I presume that you will be returning it soon; try to do so, and likewise with the enclosed and future material, since I only have the single copy."

The usual analysis and inside dope on the situation follow. I quote only the following interesting paragraphs on items that expose how the clique functions:

> "Another word re LDT. From what I hear, secretarial guards—that is, comrades who can serve both as guards and also in the other work, such as secretarial, etc.—will be required in Mexico. I think you should be considered certainly among the applicants. The period of stay would be about six months. I presume you would wish in any case to be considered when this matter comes up. I have an idea who will be the first ones selected, but still I have in mind to submit a number of comrades who would fit equally as well and probably better, as a matter of fact."

If Abern had anything to do with my being sent to Coyoacan, I thank him at this time for it. The experience there straightened a lot of things out in my mind.

> "I should like very much to know of the YPSL situation, in the Bay Region and the Los Angeles area. We hear conflicting reports. Likewise, would like a review of the State SP situation, so far as you know about it, politically and organizationally."

This was a fundamental part of the clique's organizational methods. Abern sends you the inside dope as to what is happening at the center. You in return send him the inside dope as to what is happening in your section. Then the two sets of inside dope circulate through the clique.

> "I think it is just as well to be circumspect with Barney too in talking about Cannon, myself, etc. Thru the leftwing conference, SP convention, etc., it will be possible to learn better how matters stand all around in respect to course and perspectives in the S.P. All you know is 'what you read in the papers.'"

Cannon was insisting that Barney follow party discipline in Maritime work. Barney was clearly starting out on the road which was to lead him out of the party. But Abern was not so much concerned about these particular shadings in the West Coast situation as the possibility that Barney would pass on information I might give him which would eventually reach the ears of the Political Committee. The warning was superfluous. Shortly after this I broke off all personal relations with Barney.

XIX.

I pass over a copy of a trade union and branch report sent by Widick to Swabeck, the National Secretary of the Trotskyist faction, as this was written for Cannonite consumption and therefore is of a more or less objective nature, something for the record which does not refer directly to internal problems facing the clique. It is only accidental that this report was not "returned or destroyed." And just as accidental that it did not drop into the hands of our enemies.

A letter from Abern dated January 25, 1937:

> "I would rather wait to hear from you before sending you detailed information on SP mat-

ters as they stand today. That can wait a few days if necessary till I have your forwarding address.

"Also, will you please be sure to return what material you do have to my New York address? I note you make no mention thereof, so I assume you haven't sent it on yet."

My administrative ability must have taken a decided slump at this period, for Abern insists again in the same letter:

"Be sure to send on the material you have. More anon, when I have a little more time. Have been on the go steadily since leaving NY with constant meetings."

He asks me to send the material to him in care of Albert Glotzer at Chicago; however in the very next letter he asks me to send enclosed "items" to him in care of Heisler. I presume the items would have reached him safely in care of either address.

XX.

A letter from Abern dated February 9, 1937:

"I received your lengthy letter of January 27th, but I have been so busy on this trip that I could not possibly reply any sooner. I also have the material you returned; thank you . . . I believe that the enclosed will give you a pretty good idea of happenings. But I request a special favor. It should take you but a few minutes to read the items. Therefore, will you please read quickly and *return forthwith*. I need same for other uses."

The letter continues with advice on a personal problem then facing me which I refrain from quoting and ends on the note:

"Please return enclosed *right away*."

My letter of January 27 was indeed lengthy. As I have already pointed out, the clique functions in two directions, aside from the general circulation; you pay for the inside dope from the center with reports on what is happening in your locality.

XXI.

A letter from Abern dated February 15, 1937:

"I received your letter of February 9th and by now you must have recieved material which gives you information on developments pertaining to the Appeal Institute this coming week-end, and other matters. Also, am enclosing additional material which I hope you will return quickly.

"The Institute shapes up as a very largely attended one and as one most significant for our future. I regret that California is not physically represented and I personally think that it is a grievous political error not to have found a way, despite the California Convention, to have an authoritative representative present. Cannon was to have been one of the speakers at the meeting herein referred to on the leaflet, but he signified his inability to be present."

A convention was at that time being held in California at which a sharp struggle was waged for control of the state organization. Every Trotskyist was needed there, but it gave Abern a chance for a shot from ambush at Cannon.

"I think that in respect to exchange of information, that it would be best to continue on the same basis as up till now in the past period, and that you should retain your circumspectness as before. I never for one moment gave any thought to Barney's failure in the past period to write. I took it for granted that he was very much occupied in the Maritime Strike and the editing of the Voice of the Federation, etc., and didn't expect to hear from him, as a matter of fact. Indeed, it was I, as you know, who decided that the regular methods of communication suffice in the new situation.

"Insofar as Barney may have had or still retains some subjective attitudes, I hope that they are now completely gone. As developments have shown, it was completely sound and correct for me to remain in the East undertaking the various tasks that I did, rather than to have me come to San Francisco, despite all the significance of the developments out there.

> As for Spector, as you know, I favored the idea that he take the trip, but I had no success in persuading him to do so. In respect to other aspects of the Maritime work, I think you know, and Barney, too, that I aided considerably for a number of months and together with the aid that Jack Wilson was able to give, that we helped Barney's work very considerably, so that he really should be appreciative. But as before, I think it was best to proceed as we agreed on before; particularly since I look for general improvement all around.
>
> "It is further desirable that by and large information you receive should be regarded as for yourself.
>
> "Excuse the haste. Expect to receive return of material forthwith."

One point only needs clarification. Barney and I had asked Abern to come out to the West Coast to help in the Maritime work when it first began. Abern replied that he rather favored remaining in New York but would take a poll of the boys. After the poll he informed us that it was unanimous against his coming to the West Coast. He must stay in New York where the Political Committee and the political center of the movement was located. Instead of Abern, Cannon came out to California—without the consent of the Abern clique. Looking back at this period I am now of the opinion that there was a distinct gain for us in California in having Cannon there rather than Abern.

XXII.

A letter from Abern dated February 17, 1937:

> "As respects information, etc., it seems to me it is up to the comrades in your area to ask for it. Cannon has a knowledge of affairs and developments. He should convey these informations to the comrades. It is better for Barney and others to receive their information, material, etc., through the regular channels, that it has not been forthcoming and that the B-L [Bolshevik-Leninist, that is, Trotskyist—JH] comrades in your area do not meet as a tendency to discuss and decide matters is unfortunate and wrong. Apparently California is the only locality where the need for this has not been recognized or acted upon. As for correspondence between us, that is personal between you and me, and I prefer to have it remain that way. Should Barney write us, then we can see. I have thought it no longer necessary in the circumstances because I believe the normal channels can suit the purpose and, where delinquent, improved upon. At least I hope so. As respects correspondence with Jack, that is up to Jack, but he is overloaded in the extreme. He certainly gets a lot done with his time. (I refer to correspondence with Barney; Barney is no child, but a qualified person and can make up his own mind). As for the Barney-JPC relations, the Voice, etc., I guess that Barney built up some illusions in his mind and now is a bit depressed thereby; but there's plenty of time to get one's feet on the ground again, and, as you say, what is required is a perspective and organization and activities for the carrying out of same.
>
> "An additional word now and reply to your letters at another time. Yes, there is basic accord among the leading comrades in the East, Chicago, other points as to basic tasks and perspectives in the next period. It has nothing to do with an evaluation of the value of the entry into the S.P. etc. Agreement concerns itself with the tasks to be carried out, now that we are in (and it is hard to say how long we can remain, for anything can happen). Our common outlook consists essentially in the need to press forward more rapidly now with our program, including the raising of the issue of the New International.
>
> "The divisions between Cannon and the rest of the Center have been important; the matter of Labor Action was but incidental and disagreement was of a practical character, easy to resolve. Political questions, perspective and organizational methods were involved and on every main issue, the Center has been proved correct. It would take altogether too long to go into the past controversy at this time, nor do I think it particularly necessary. Suffice that the Committee was pretty sharp with what it regarded as manifestations of Molinierism on C's part. But the center aimed all the time to lessen the differences and to arrive at an understanding. Time has made this possible, or

so we think and we see no reason why there should be anything but unity everywhere on the next main tasks of the B-L forces.

"More anon. Please return enclosed material quickly to my New York address."

I was coming more and more to the opinion that the anti-entrists had been completely in error—the living reality of concrete events was demonstrating this before my eyes—and hence I was re-evaluating the roles of all those who had figured in the previous faction struggle. At the same time my personal loyalty to Abern made me hope and wish that this friction between him and Cannon could be liquidated and the party genuinely united. If Abern would re-evaluate his estimate of the entry, it seemed to me that the basis would then be formed for this desirable liquidation of the friction. I did not yet understand that the Abern clique can commit no errors.

XXIII

A few highlights from a letter from Abern dated March 1, 1937:

> "The Socialist Appeal, which should be out in a few days, will no doubt carry an adequate report on the main aspects of the Appeal Institute and I do not believe I need go into that here to any extent. I am sorry that you were unable to be present; it would have been more than worth-while. The enclosed copy (please return forthwith) gives you a few brief observations of this and that. Glotzer, Widick, Natie, myself, and others were active figures at the Institute and more than measured up to the requirements . . ."

In the night world of the Abern clique, there are no "requirements" that are not lived up to.

> "We hear all sorts of rumors about California; the SP convention and so on. Perhaps you could enlighten me."

As a loyal clique member, I enlightened him.

> "It does not seem to be very difficult to get to see LDT, in case it becomes possible for you to get down there at some time. Ruthie Ageloff, visiting Mexico, also got to see him and no doubt has lived vicariously ever since."

The leaders of the opposition will no doubt correct me promptly if I am mistaken in my impression that Ruthie Ageloff stayed down there for several months subsequently.

> "Apropos SP entry, etc., I dealt with this in a few lines in my previous letter, and, come to think of it, there is little to add thereto. Matters are coming to a head rather swiftly. We have to try to get what we can. This SP which was to grow by the thousands (JPC thesis) has perhaps 6,000 members divided into god only knows how many tendencies and groups. Essentially the issue in the SP is a struggle for domination by either the Stalinist or Trotskyist ideology. We have to fight every inch of the way for our views, regardless of what the organizational results or forms are to be. As respects what was, my views have remained the same. The comrades who thought the entry invalid entered into the work nevertheless with a will and have, and I think done the most effective work. Chicago, for instance, is probably the best of the left wing movements, both in the SP and YPSL. Elsewhere we have worked with similar effects."

This paragraph indicates very clearly that although the Abern clique no longer officially existed it nevertheless was cooperative in its organized underground manner in working within the Socialist Party without any factional hangovers.

The letter refers to clique member Earle Robertson of Canada (Abern's clique has international connections) and asks me by "all means get in touch with him, and then let's hear what is what." I had heard that Robertson had resigned from the Fourth International and inasmuch as he was the man who had won me over to the Fourth International and the Abern clique I was interested in what he did even more than in the case of A. J. Muste.

The letter ends:

"Please acknowledge receipt of letters quickly and also return items sent you previously, Etc."

XXIV.

A letter from Abern dated March 5, 1937:

"Enclosed some recent material issued on SP situation. Presume you'll get it later, but am sending it on anyhow."

A brief analysis of the situation in the SP follows and then:

"I understand that Cannon will be in New York before going on to the SP convention, in which case there will be the opportunity for some Club meetings with all forces at hand to review and to outline next tasks.

"From Max's letter I note that you expect to move to B.'s address. Where do you want mail sent in that event? I prefer to another address. How about continuance of the present one? More anon."

Cannon was watched at all times by the clique the same way a flock of chickens watch a fox outside the pen. When he took a trip anywhere it was duly reported. I am sure that Abern at any moment, night or day, could at least name the town in which Cannon happened to be staying if not the exact address.

XXV.

I now quote from a carbon copy of a letter of mine to Abern dated March 5, 1937 in order better to understand a reference made in one of Abern's subsequent letters to me:

"Cannon has been talking a good deal about discipline among the B-L's, particularly concerning Barney, so I suppose the NC still has a beef with Barney over past matters. But that beef will have to be settled between them. All I know is what went on around the paper, and I thought Barney did a pretty good job."

It is not correct that all I knew was what "went on around the paper." Barney had taken the editorship without consulting the Political Committee, thereby violating discipline and eventually inflicting heavy damage on the party. I did not want to become involved in this as I was vulnerable myself on this score; and Cannon had succeeded in pounding into my skull by this time that such a violation of discipline was serious. I wished to avoid the consequences of a crime I had not realized I was committing at the time. Like all the Abernites I was more anxious to bury the past where it hurt than to learn from it.

That Cannon had more trust in me than I had in him was shown by the fact that he asked me to work on the staff of Labor Action, later leaving me virtually in charge. At the same time in the branch such vicious Cannonites as Weiss pushed me into taking a post as organizer. All the other Abernites in the branch took this activity of mine as a sign that I had capitulated to Cannon. I can still feel the shock of surprise I got when my clique members started to snipe at me on the branch floor as a turncoat, Weiss at the back of the room smiling to himself. He had gone through the same process not long before.

XXVI.

A letter from Abern dated March 13, 1937:

"I have yours of the 5th and 9th. It is unfortunate that Labor Action has run into financial difficulties just at this time, prior to the national convention. Some money, fifty dollars or more, besides a hundred for Cannon, was sent to Labor Action a few days ago from here. And a few weeks back, a couple of hundred or more was sent. This was handled through our center and quite probably has been handled at your end in a special manner, so in case you are not aware of the above, please keep the information strictly to yourself. At any rate what can be done from here is being done; but finally Labor Action will have, in my opinion, to depend on its own sources of support, that is, in the West and kin area . . . Here there is the matter of the Appeal, which I think must come first in our needs; we are having a hard time getting out the Institute issue, which is so important for us. Naturally the Appeal Institute took most of our resources everywhere, and despite extreme economies we have a deficit to make up as the enclosed will show. Am sending you a copy just for information purposes. Vincent Dunne writes, in commending the organization work of us for the Institute, etc., that he is surprised that the deficit is so low, in view of the scope of the gathering and so on. Well, you know, it's the Abern in one."

Note the insinuation that Cannon has taken for himself funds ear marked for Labor Action. If I had not known already from the sudden flux of food in the Cannon cupboard, the new hat and topcoat Cannon bought from a second-hand clothing store, and his preparations for a trip to New York which required money from the Political Committee, I could well have gone on thinking to this day that Cannon was not altogether strict about what happened to party funds.

> "Just what line, if any, was followed by Cannon in California, many are anxious to learn. What you have to say on this or that phase of California activities helps but I imagine that there will be quite a few queries. My own impression is that in some other places there was less noise and ballyhoo but better and more lasting results, as in Chicago, Ohio."

Chicago and Ohio, these were the bright-spots of the Abern clique.

> "As for the talk of discipline, etc., you mention, well, I'm not sure but that the one who is complaining of others will have first to take a good look at himself, in view of the questions that arose in the past period."

Will the leaders of the opposition permit me to believe that I have established enough facts to label this remark of Abern's as at least hypocritical?

XXVII.

A letter from Abern dated March 14, 1937:

> "Enclosed is a copy of minutes of proceedings of the Appeal Institute. They will add at least outlines of the Institute. The Socialist Appeal containing a review of the Institute is now out and no doubt copies will soon be in your hands.
>
> "Please return the enclosed copy forthwith. It is in reply to a couple of questions on recent developments and I have nothing I could particularly add now. As you will note I believe that we will come out of the convention all right. As to what will follow and what will be our course immediately thereafter, I'm hardly in a position to say until there have been discussions and until we have seen just what policies, rules, program and so on the convention adopts. I doubt that others who have not been constantly on the scene of developments here, in Chicago, etc. can add anything of importance by way of analysis and what is next to be done."

The reference to "others" who could add nothing of "importance by way of analysis" I took to mean Cannon. Perhaps Abern if he checks through the files of his correspondence with his non-existent group can enlarge on this point.

XXVIII.

From a letter of mine to Abern dated March 26, 1937:

> "I think it a good precaution if in your correspondence with me you leave off the notation PERSONAL on the envelope of your mail. No one else opens my mail anyway and that notation makes it too conspicuous. Also your initials and address are rather well known. If you could use another name and address such as Sterling's it would be preferable."

Some comrades who were not members of the Abern clique were staying with me at the time. I was only taking the elementary precautions required of all members of the Abern clique in hiding the existence of the group and its ramifications.

XXIX.

A letter from Abern dated April 5, 1937:

This letter gives the inside dope on what occurred at the SP convention held at Chicago. The following paragraphs give Abern's conclusions:

"Even more specifically I am more concerned, although the formalities had been complied with C-S, with thc fact that in actual practice Glotzer, myself, and others, were not consulted or matters discussed with, during the proceedings even though the situation was such as would have easily produced accord on the questions as they arose. In short, what the ranks resented, some of us could even more so. I took part in the Appeal and other meetings to the extent that was possible and necessary, as did Glotzer and others. There were 'informal' talks at various hours, which serve purposes just as well, often better, than formal ones, but I and others were not in them. Whether with intent or otherwise, and I am disposed to put the best face on it, such exclusions are unwise and will prove unfortunate if continued. C-S, particularly the former, had better learn some things more quickly; the resentment of the ranks is a sign that comrades all want to be treated in a much healthier fashion. I minimize these matters in the hope some of these manifestations, which are a continuance of past practices, and which are entirely unjustified in view of the essential accord for the next tasks, will be corrected soon, beginning at the top. I send even this brief comment for your own information to indicate that certain problems remain despite improvements, that I have mentioned same in the proper places, and am willing to wait to see how things develop."

It would seem that of Cannon and Shachtman, the latter learned things "more quickly." He is now an attorney for the Abern clique. The remark about the justifiableness of "informal meetings" is of significance in view of the present cries of the opposition about the now famous "New Years Day meeting."

XXX.

A letter from Abern dated April 9, 1937:

"Enclosed are a couple more items by way of information.

"Cannon, I understand, is still in Chicago. How long he will remain I don't know.

"In a letter of yours to Max St. which I read, you mention that the Clarity people seem elated over the convention. Well, don't take that too seriously. They are the ones who suffered most politically, as time will show. What they have is a fictitious, not real, control, and they are going to have plenty of headaches, with their political and organizational vacillations. . . . I am not concerned about the Clarity elements, nor the other groupings, but more with our own forces. Perspectives in the next days have to be made more clear and simply understood; I hope this can be done—probably will, because too events will pull the stolid or placid from their seats. But believe me, Joe, certain internal aspects, manner of functioning, etc. will have to be remedied quickly, or there will be difficulties."

Trotsky was not the only one who foresaw difficulties, although it is true enough he ascribed it to the petty bourgeois composition of the party and its lack of theoretical development rather than to "high-handed ways" as Abern describes it in this same letter.

Abern asks about Barney and adds:

"I've thought of dropping him a personal note."

The letter ends with the clique's motto on administrative efficiency:

"I would be obliged if you would *really* return items quickly, and of course keep in confidence, as hitherto. . . ."

The Abernites always reacted most sharply and sensitively to administrative questions such as this. There was no crime greater than laxness over returning items about confidential happenings unless it was exposing the existence of the clique.

XXXI.

A letter from Abern dated April 13, 1937:

"A note from a Chicago comrade mentions that JPC made some casual remarks about

Hansen-Abern relations, intimating, I presume, something about correspondence or trying to ascertain something. Presumably the conversation concerned itself briefly with matter of liquidating remnants of factional hang-overs. Well, we'll see; my suggestion to you is to be circumspect in conversations. And of course correspondence between us is strictly for us. . . . More later on happenings, activities, etcetera. . . . Meanwhile will you send on the items you were to return? thanks.

"Cannon, you probably know, is back on the coast, in Los Angeles. He has a leave of absence for a couple of months in effort for health improvement.

"With Comrade Cannon in LA, is the editorship of Labor Action to be left in your hands? From what I observed of Trimble, I wouldn't count very much on him; politically a light weight, and further one who is likely to pull fast ones, as he had already in Chicago."

Trimble, now in the opposition, has of course since that time gained considerably in political weight. The Chicago remark of Cannon mentioned above was to enjoy wide discussion in the Abern clique—a storm in the depths without a ripple on the formal surface of nonexistence.

XXXII.

A letter from Max Sterling dated April 29, 1937.

"By this time all the California delegates must have returned from the national convention and I trust that now you know something about the goings on there. In any case I am sending you the enclosed document in the form of a letter to a comrade. I believe the thing was written by Shachtman and is more or less correct. In addition there were occurrences behind the scenes of the convention which in so far as it relates to the Appeal tendency are not so flattering. I understand (I was not present at the convention) that there was a virtual rebellion on the part of the Appeal rank and filers at the convention against the Appeal leadership for facing them at all turns with a fait accomplis and that there was a feeling on the part of these lowlies that things were done without them having a say in their doing. Not that these things were done wrongly, in most cases they were not, but that they were done shall we say high handedly. Things must have been pretty extreme in this respect if most of the members of the club found themselves in the same position as the rank and filers. I do not say that Cannon and Shachtman did this deliberately to the others but I do believe that this is unfortunately part of the makeup of people whose qualities do not run along organizational lines, people who are prone to work by themselves in their capacity of journalist or orator. It is not necessary to add that among those who received the cold shoulder was Marty but in his case the thing may not have been entirely unconscious. In this respect there is an incident which is only too revealing. After the convention was over, Cannon, who was ill, remained over in Chicago. During his stay there he was visited by Norman Satir who discussed with him a number of things. After a while Cannon's mood became very confidential and out of a clear sky he expressed himself thus: "You know Norman I've been thinking seriously of proposing Marty for secretary of the Club.' 'What stands in the way Jim?' says Norman and Cannon replies 'Well I think Marty is still an intriguer even after our entry into the SP.' Norman presses him 'What proof is there of this Jim?' Cannon replies very vaguely about Marty and the coast, about Marty and Hansen. 'Still,' says Cannon, 'I am thinking seriously about doing away with all factional reminiscences and proposing Marty for secretary.'

"Does not this conversation reveal who it is that has had a factional and discriminatory attitude up to now? In the meantime Arne has left NY in order to find work and take up residence in Chicago and Joe Carter has replaced him as secretary at least for the time being. What is hopeful about the above conversation is that at last we may be considered as first class citizens. Why is Cannon having a change of mind? One can only guess. My own opinion is that Cannon realizes that Marty is an extremely valuable person especially now when most of our weaknesses are of an organizational nature. It is possible that Marty may make some order out of the organizational chaos that exists and that threatens to fall down upon our heads. Furthermore Cannon must be convinced that Marty has acted in a non-factional way ever since the entry. Add to this that the relations between Cannon and Shachtman-Burnham are none too good which of course tends to break down the reality of a closed corporation."

Sterling's letter sheds light on the Shachtman brief that he and Cannon acted like Siamese twins in the past period. Was Shachtman evincing a petty-bourgeois tendency then?

Sterling reports the excellent work Abern has been accomplishing at the Ohio State convention of the S. P.

> "We certainly deserved to win this state for practically all the active forces and the best mass workers are our own. How it turns out, from what Marty reports from Ohio, that we would be lucky to get parity with the Clarityites. And why? Only because fellows like Cochrane, Selander, and Pollack were so sure that we were going to stay in the SP for such a hell of a time, that we would work our way up so gradually that they became completely immersed in mass work to the utter neglect of their SP duties. Virtually only the Akron boys were on the job and if we get 7 delegates out of 35 they will be the ones plus Marty, who has been running around like a madman there, that we will have to thank."

The scene shifts to New York!

> "Experience here has demonstrated that at least at this stage our tendency can not function properly except in some organized form and this we have done informally. We have sent Clarke and Harold Robbins out to Detroit as field organizers but it is perhaps even more important that NY have a full time organizer. In NY, because it is the most difficult place to crack, he would have to be an exceptionally fine organizer which brings us straight to Marty Abern. For a long time this has been in the back of my head and now that Marty is psychologically prepared to accept such a job at least such is my belief and the others are beginning to see that there is no other way out, the chances are good that this may be achieved."

It was to require the assistance of Burnham and Shachtman, the trading away of dialectical materialism, defense of the Soviet Union, and democratic centralism before Sterling's wish could come true. The letter does not end on the optimistic note of Sterling's wish but with the usual Abern clique refrain:

> "Marty sends his best regards to you and asks that you return some items he sent you."

XXXIII.

A letter from Abern dated April 26, 1937:

After discussing the question of the fight over Barney's editorship, which he had now shifted to the American Newspaper Guild, Abern closes:

> "We won a big victory at the Ohio state convention. We may be congratulated. See enclosed herein, and/or other items to follow. Actually it was fortunate I was sent out, or the task wouldn't have been accomplished, I know."

As I have pointed out before the clique lives in a dream world in which the revolution revolves around the mighty deeds and mighty abilities of its members, especially Abern's.

XXXIV.

During May of 1937 I more clearly expressed the direction in which I was traveling and the correspondence from Abern became more circumspect although its analyses are just as long-winded. I detect a defensive tone—slight, but nevertheless there. The letters invariably end with the note: "Try to return the material I sent you at the earliest opportunity." There is more discussion of what Cannon said to Satir in Chicago, what it meant, information about a tour of Shachtman, of Rosmer being in New York ("this is confidential.") Discussions about Labor Action and seeming agreement as to its role, high commendation of Natie Gould's work in Chicago, discussions of the fight with the Clarityites and the issues involved. We come to June 16, 1937, with a blast against Cannon from Max Sterling (after the usual analysis of negotiations, maneuvers, and the progress of the faction fight in the SP which was heading toward expulsion of the left wing).

> "In the midst of all this the Old Man, without knowing of these developments but basing himself on Shachtman's analysis of the last convention, has expressed himself very sharply on our course in the SP. He takes Shachtman to task for stating that the convention was a big step forward in view of its real attitude on the people's front as it is expressed in Wisconsin and its shameful position or lack of a position on Spain. The Old Man draws the conclusion that we are adapting ourselves dangerously to the centrists and what is needed is a straight-out fight in the party especially on Spain and the Moscow Trials. He observes that the SP is a very poor party with a very poor composition and that it may well nigh prove to be impossible of capturing while to set ourselves this task may prove to be a fatal illusion. He demands a sharp turn be the consequences what they may.
>
> "The situation in NY forms a very good background for the favorable assimilation of this advice and there are very few comrades indeed who have not come around to this way of thinking. It was good to see that in a very recent letter from Cannon he too has reacted to the Old Man's letter in the same way as we here. In fact Cannon makes the letter his own program not only of the present but also of the past. He claims he advised Shachtman against the analysis he made of the convention. Whatever may be the truth of this claim elementary honesty demands that if mistakes were made Cannon too participated in them for who does not remember Cannon's last trip to NY where he appeared as the dove of peace as against the wild men from NY. And earlier than that who was it that constantly cautioned us to go slow, ever so slow? I must say that I am a little sickened by this show of infallibility from he who should lay the least claim to it so far as our entry into the SP is concerned with all the exaggerated claims that would result from this step and so far as our actual course in the SP is concerned."

This letter referred to above by Sterling was a highly confidential communication which had no business circulating outside of the Political Committee, yet here is Max Sterling a rank and filer passing on the inside information to me out in California another rank and filer. I have often wondered how the clique got a copy of this letter. Were copies passed out to the members of the Political Committee, including Abern? Was a copy sent to Abern from the household of the author?

XXXV.

A letter from Abern dated June 19, 1937:

The usual inside information about the progress of the factional struggle. The following paragraph is of interest:

> "Please regard the items enclosed as *very confidential*, just for your own information. I would have preferred that the letters and issues referred to had not come into being, but being as they did, there was nothing else to do, I suppose, but to state the facts. There was no excuse for any buck-passing. My hope is that the matter will now be regarded as questions of the past and that we can go forward with the truly pressing issues before us. All the comrades sharply resented the inexcusable, and false, attempt of the initiator to pass the buck. Haven't these items, but will try to obtain and send on for your information. I think you should know about these things, if only for your own knowledge."

What is the meaning of these unusually cryptic words? The enclosed items were copies of correspondence between Cannon and Burnham. Making them available to me, a rank and filer, was equivalent to asking my judgement in a dispute that had not been taken out of the Political Committee and which was not later taken out of the Committee. But then as a member with full rights in the nonexistent Abern clique this inside dope was just part of my ordinary privileges.

However, factional differences, to believe Abern, are being eliminated bit by bit in this period except of course for the factionalism of Cannon and all the hand-raisers who were not in our clique. (From the previous correspondence cited above, it would seem that in this period Cannon was the only Cannonite on the Political Committee. The others all saw eye to eye.)

> "Aside: I don't take too seriously Cannon's private remarks re myself and the Appeal. It's a matter he thought of in Chicago too after the SP convention. Well, we'll see how the new party set-up, when it emerges, shows up. In the East—NY—we've pretty well cracked old alignments and are concerning ourselves as objectively as possible with issues as they arise. I refer to those who have some independence of thought and character. Boston is about the only place I know of where ex-C-S people stir up dirt and crudities. Maybe it's the old Puritan habit. Anyhow, I'm not greatly exercised thereby."

Note that those with independence of thought and character inevitably end up in the Abern clique. This was as true in the pre-entry struggles, and in the nonexistent days as it is today in the present struggle. You can always tell an Abernite by his aura of dynamic and independent thought.

> "P. S.—Possibly not all the stuff sent from the Center gets to you, since sometimes it's used only in NY (in one or two instances, I think). If you'll send me a list of the stuff you've received, I'll check & send any missing material."

Trust Abern to look after the administrative details.

XXXVI.

A letter from Abern dated June 24, 1937:

> "Enclosed are the items you wanted to read; thanks for same. They read well. Enclosed, too, are a couple of things emanating from Chicago to add to your picture of affairs in the Party. Oblige by returning soon, please. Other items to follow in couple of days.
>
> "Thru a Boston comrade I glean the following information that may interest you casually. A letter from Crary Trimble to a Boston comrade quotes her as saying that she is very much disappointed with our (WP) people on the west coast. Says that those who were against the entry are actually pitching in and working in a number of ways as 'real revolutionists,' but the others she calls 'intellectual masturbators.' Regards Cannon as a good leader, dislikes Goldman. Says the Cannonites look upon her and Glen as something 'they' may accept in the future; then cries, 'when the hell do they become kosher.'
>
> "A sailor comrade from the coast beaching on the Atlantic a while ago says 'Cannon gets along very good with Barney Mayes, because Jim can get along with anyone (sic!), *but* Jim has told us all what he really thinks of Barney.' What does this mean, Joe?
>
> "Shachtman has been in Frisco till now, I believe. Am interested to know how things panned out, what he had to say, your impressions, etc."

This is another prominent feature of the Abern clique. Along with the endless "items" of confidential information little bits of spicy gossip keep the dish hot and peppery. But this letter does indicate that the opposition charge that an "'anti-intellectuals' attitude is drummed into the minds of party members" by the "Cannon clique" would seem to be incorrect, at least in the case of the Trimbles.

The Left Wing of the SP was now being expelled by Thomas, and everyone was doing his utmost to unite our ranks for a stiff fight against those expulsions. The former members of the Workers Party for their part—at least as individuals—were adding up the results of the entry. I had now come to the definitive conclusion that the entry had been correct and that my opposition had been completely incorrect, that I had under-estimated the possibilities in the SP and because of provincial isolation had completely over-estimated our own numerical strength prior to entry. (I had thought there were at least 5,000 Trotskyites in the United States after scaling down my original low estimates, when I first joined, that there were probably not more than 25 or 30 thousand). But my most serious mistake was getting inveigled into the Abern clique. In this clique I became tied to an individual leader rather than a set of principles. It is only proper that I here express my gratitude to the Marxist pedagogues who subsequently cut me loose from individual leaders as such and replaced them with the Marxist method of arriving at political positions.

XXXVII.

A letter from Abern dated June 25, 1937:

> "*Important*: Have sent you quite a few things in recent days. Please read at once and return to me, and, of course, keep *strictly confidential*."

Abern was naturally worried about my delay in returning the very interesting Cannon-Burnham correspondence. Double under-lines and even single under-lines are not unusual in his letters. They are Abern's way of expressing deep emotion!

XXXVIII.

A letter from Abern dated June 28, 1937:

> "A few words re the C-Burn. letters and W's [the very important confidential letter—JH]—and then schluss on my part. The W. letter was of May 25th; it takes a couple of days for same to arrive in the States. The C. letters were of June 9 and 10th. So some ten days after the W. letter, there appears in the C. letters this sharp turn on perspective. So much for that. . . . What is important is that the leading comrades from coast to coast appear to have a common line on the next steps and perspective, apart from incidentals. That is decisive. Anent the C-B letters, I was the one who was opposed to sending them out to the club members, for the reason that I thought they might do harm to the future work, at a time when, whatever we thought of how matters were disposed of in the past year, we had accord on present and future tasks. It was others who insisted they go out; maybe the air is cleared thereby; I don't know, but I hope so. I am in accord with you absolutely that we should endeavor to compose differences in the leadership at this stage, when we are confronting the combined Right-Centrist enemies. I think we can and will—at the coming plenum of our forces. The past can be evaluated at another time, so far as necessary. Now we have to carry through unitedly the struggle against Rights and Centrists."

That Cannon is a tail-endist to Trotsky is one of the oldest slogans on the underground banner of the Abern clique. No opportunity is allowed to slip by that will "prove" it.

XXXIX.

A letter from Abern dated July 10, 1937:

After mentioning that a "young sailor" (Blackie Johnson) "was here last week for a few days and I and others talked with him a good deal and got a more intimate picture of the maritime set-up," Abern informs me that Barney has re-established connections with the clique center and "would like to hear from us and so on. First direct note from them in about a year, I guess. Has he gotten back into any activity in the SP?"

The letter ends:

> "Believe you have an item or two yet of mine. . . . Cannon and Shachtman are due back in New York in a few days."

That Abern could re-establish relations with Barney shocked me even after this long experience in his clique. After folding up at the end of the first round with the Stalinists just when he should have begun a more intensive campaign against them, no one on the West Coast was more thoroughly discredited in our eyes than Barney. That connections were re-established between Abern and Barney is clearly shown in the letter from Abern dated July 15, 1937:

After the usual analysis of internal occurrences:

> "Anent Barney. I am told that he maintained touch with the maritime convention at Portland by telephone and telegram, and that if there had been any opportunity to have had a chance to make clear what was involved in

the Voice fight, he would by all means have been there—So there you are—On the other hand your information is too pertinent to be ignored. . . ."

This is sheer mis-information. Barney had refused both a request from the progressive trade union forces to go to Portland and a steering committee decision of the Bay area that he go. With a majority of the progressives at the convention Barney would have been granted not only the floor to defend his editorship of the Voice against the Stalinists but would have been reinstated in all likelihood as editor. He predicted that the progressives would be in a minority—an inexcusable miscalculation and in any case an unprincipled position—and hence refused to go to the convention, leaving the progressives holding the bag.

> "By the way, evaluation of the entry? An endless argument that can never be settled. My own position is even more categoric than it ever was, for a dozen or more reasons I'm not going into here. Should the question arise for discussion, I'll certainly express my opinions. Never having been against the entry on principle, I can only add and subtract as to gains and losses, and in my judgment the losses are greater than any benefits that have shown themselves—very much so. And this is without consideration of the original and heavily decorated reasons for the entry by C-S: namely, a growth to 15,–20,000 members, left-ward moving (exploding as surely as the Zeppelin); capturing the party—which motivated our tactics during the past year or more; rather it is a split, perhaps three ways or more, that is resulting. . . . My concern is how are we going to carry on from here."

And with that Abern buried the question of the entry and the lessons to be learned from this most important organizational turn of the Fourth Internationalists in the United States.

In August of 1937 I came to New York. In conversation with me, Abern expanded on the above thesis. It was clear beyond all doubt that he had learned absolutely nothing from the entry experience. He was bitter about being "framed," as he put it, by someone of the Cannonites sending an important letter to an enemy address on the eve of the split. I talked with another important Abernite. He wanted to know if I still felt the way the rest of the boys did about Cannon and the entry. When I responded that my experience working with Cannon in California had convinced me that we had incorrectly estimated his role, his ideas, and his methods in the movement, the Abernite looked depressed and the conversation died away with vague references to the "psychological uneasiness" one felt walking with a silent Cannon down the street, the hope that Abern would be recognized and given a post that would permit Abern's strong organizational points to make up for Cannon's weaknesses. That was the end of my membership in the Abern clique. I graduated into the ranks of the party.

In my previous article I commented on the significance of what had happened to all the former prominent individuals who had been connected with Abern, Muste going back to the church, Sneevliet to the London Bureau, Spector and Barney into retirement from politics, only Weber back into the proletarian wing of the party. There was one other instructive example which I did not include for the simple reason that his break from the Abern clique had not yet occurred: I refer to the case of Earle Robertson.[2]

Robertson started as a professor who joined the C. P. in the third period days and then split a group away from it to form a branch in Salt Lake in 1933. After the frenzy of third period politics in the C. P. where revolution was breaking out in every event that made headlines in the world press, the Trotskyist group no doubt seemed "conservative" to Robertson eager to drown his doubts in the most violent kind of activity. In this period at least, the responsiveness to the cry about Cannon's "conservatism" can be explained in a measure as a hang-

2. Earl Robertson was the pen name of Earle Birney. After leaving the Trotskyist movement, he devoted himself to literary activities, becoming one of Canada's best-known poets.—JH (1972).

over of ultra-leftism in those who came from the Stalinist party of the third period. It was Robertson who presented Trotskyism to me and along with it, without making any distinction—Abernism. He spent some years in England where he was active in the movement, visited Trotsky in Norway, was beaten by Nazis in Germany while touring there, had the reputation of being one of the leaders of the Canadian movement, was prominent in the Canadian press of the Fourth International. He was never able to make up his mind to leave the professorial world and his career there for the highly uncertain life of a professional revolutionist. Although he is a very intelligent and gifted man, it is now clear that he had never grasped *dialectical* materialism, never understood either Bolshevik theory or practise. Upon resigning from the Fourth International on January 12, 1940, he stated:

> "It is with deepest regret that I have come to decide that I can no longer continue as a member of the Socialist Workers League. The reasons are not simple and not entirely political. They are chiefly these:
>
> "1. I have no confidence in the present leadership either here or in the United States, and I have no longer full confidence in the international leadership. It is not simply a matter of my being at the moment in a minority position on the Buro on the Finnish question. I have often been in a minority position. I have opposed the Cannon leadership ever since I became a member of the American section in 1933 . . . Today it is a matter of feeling that the SWL does not contain within its membership the necessary leadership. I do not want to replace the present Buro with others, for I have still less confidence in the others. I feel that a rev. organization must have a leadership which is able to think for itself, independently, creatively. I do not think that, since the retirement of MacDonald and Spector, we have had such a leadership. I have now lost faith that it can be developed out of the available material. Events may prove me wrong, and I hope so."

He continues with *Burnham's* position about the seeds of Stalinism being latent in the Bolshevik organization and that these seeds are already sown in the 4th International. He rejects defense of the USSR in any kind of war, feeling that capitalism is no worse than what "seems to be there" and ends up most significantly:

> "I know my position has many weaknesses. It is partly a tiredness, I suppose—partly middle class isolation and despair, no doubt—but I can't get out of it, and the best thing to do is to face it."

He denies in his last paragraph that his resignation is due to the outbreak of war and the resulting pressure. An Abernite can show no weakness even when he starts toward the camp of the bourgeoisie.

Robertson epitomizes the whole development of the Abern clique from 1933 to date—petty-bourgeois isolation from the working class and despair ending up with a fit of the blues and Burnham's bourgeois morality.

I have proved I think conclusively enough to convince the more fair-minded members of the opposition—the leaders are thoroughly familiar with the role of Abern—that far from dissolving itself at the time of the entry into the Socialist Party, Abern's clique—at least its basic cadres—simply went underground. Not all the different ways of crying "liar" in the vocabulary of the clique's present attorneys can cover up that fact.

May I now be permitted a few conclusions from the mass of evidence I have presented? I charged that in our party a certain group maintained an artificial existence by feeding on information slipped down to them through a grapevine from a certain member of the Political Committee. I think that I have substantiated this charge. I charged that the main characteristic of this group was its placing wholly secondary and less than secondary questions above political principles. I think that I have substantiated this charge. I charged that this group maintained itself by organizational methods that are incompatible with Bolshevism. I think that I have substantiated this charge. I charged that of the organizational schools in our party, Abern's has proved to be the most costly, especially in relation to the youth. I think that I have substantiated this charge. I charged that this group constituted the core of the present opposition. I think that I have substantiated this charge. While Burnham and Shachtman were making a peace treaty on philosophy in order to unite on a political deviation from Marxism, the Abern clique—I believe I have established this now *factually*—was patiently biding its time to utilize them as fronts in a renewed campaign against the party "regime." The war crisis touched off the powder which flared up in our party as the petty-bourgeois opposition.

Comrade Trotsky remarked in his article "A Petty-Bourgeois Opposition in the Socialist Workers Party" that "it is possible to say that Burnham and Shachtman are the amateurs of the opposition while Abern is the unquestionable professional." The full meaning of this remark is clear I believe in the light of the above quotations from the correspondence of the Abern clique. If there was ever a cult that believed in its leader, it is the Abern cult. Consider: against the defection of Muste, Spector, Sneevliet, Robertson, against the warning of Weber, the admonitions and arguments of Cannon for ten years, Shachtman for a briefer period, and now the sharpest and most categoric analysis of their role from Leon Trotsky—together with a political bankruptcy proved a thousand times over by events—these people still cling to Abern. All these blows should make them at least doubtful about the infallibility of his leadership one would think. Still they cling to Abern.

This is perhaps explainable, at least in part, by the fact that Abern expresses the weaknesses of the petty-bourgeois layers in our party better than anyone else. He consoles their wounded vanities, their hurt prides, their frustrated ambitions; he organizes a little world for them in which they revolve in a sort of perpetual motion, flattering each other, sympathizing with each other, laughing, joking, nourished on bits of gossip and scandal about the Political Committee, the general staff—and all the while they bask in the aura of revolution and the Fourth International.

If the opposition splits from the party, do Burnham and Shachtman imagine that they will constitute the leadership of this group? Do they imagine that they can take over a clique which is able to go underground for years at a time, leading a feverish and active ambush existence while officially maintaining the pretense that they are nothing but a phantasy? Burnham and Shachtman, especially Shachtman, are organizational captives of Abern just as he is their ideological captive. And this monstrosity thinks it has a future as an independent group!

So far as the Fourth International is concerned, in my estimation the departure of these people if they intend to persist as a clique, could be counted only as a gain. Those individuals who are in the opposition by mistake will find their way back to the Fourth International when they have had a better chance to see the Abern clique in action in *open* opposition to the proletarian party that will represent the Fourth International in the United States.

MARCH 24, 1940

COMMUNIST CONTINUITY AND PROGRAM

New!

The Fight Against Jew-Hatred and Pogroms in the Imperialist Epoch

Stakes for the International Working Class

V.I. LENIN, LEON TROTSKY
FARRELL DOBBS
JAMES P. CANNON
JACK BARNES
DAVE PRINCE

Jew-hatred and pogroms—like Hamas carried out on October 7, 2023—are now part of the permanent social convulsions and wars of the imperialist epoch. That's why fighting Jew-hatred is of decisive importance to the working class and oppressed nations of the entire world. The authors answer the all-important question: What is to be done to end it—for all time. $10. Also in Spanish, soon in French.

Are They Rich Because They're Smart?

Class, Privilege, and Learning under Capitalism

JACK BARNES

Exposes growing class inequalities in the US and the self-serving rationalizations of well-paid professionals who think their "brilliance" equips them to "regulate" working people, who don't know what's in our own best interest. $10. Also in Spanish, French, Farsi, Arabic.

The Third International after Lenin

LEON TROTSKY

Leon Trotsky's 1928 defense of the Marxist course that had guided the Communist International in its early years. Writing in the heat of political battle, Trotsky addresses the key challenge facing working people today: building communist parties throughout the world capable of leading workers and farmers to take power. $20. Also in Farsi.

Cuba and the Coming American Revolution

JACK BARNES

This is a book about the example set by the Cuban people that socialist revolution is not only necessary—it can be made. A book about the struggles of workers and other exploited producers in the imperialist heartland, and the youth attracted to them. About the class struggle in the US, where the revolutionary capacities of working people are as utterly discounted by the ruling powers as were those of the Cuban toilers. And just as wrongly. $10. Also in Spanish, French, Farsi.

In Defense of Marxism

Against the Petty-Bourgeois Opposition in the Socialist Workers Party

LEON TROTSKY

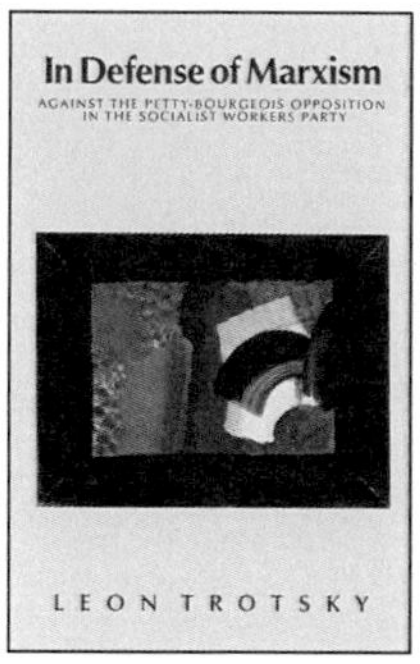

A reply to those in the revolutionary workers movement in the late 1930s buckling to bourgeois patriotism during Washington's buildup to enter World War II. Trotsky explains why only a party fighting to bring workers into its ranks and leadership can steer a communist course. In the process, he defends the materialist and dialectical foundations of Marxism. $17. Also in Spanish and French.

The Struggle for a Proletarian Party

JAMES P. CANNON

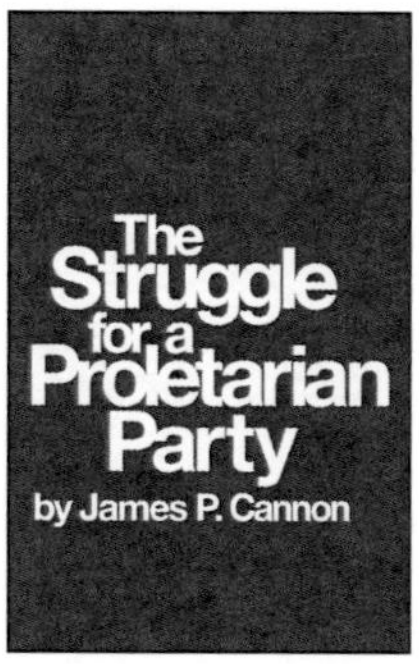

"The workers of America have power enough to topple the structure of capitalism at home and to lift the whole world with them when they rise," Cannon asserts. On the eve of World War II, a founder of the communist movement in the US and leader of the Communist International in Lenin's time defends the program and party-building norms of Bolshevism. $20. Also in Spanish and Farsi.

Revolutionary Continuity

Marxist Leadership in the U.S.

The Early Years, 1848–1917

Birth of the Communist Movement, 1918–1922

FARRELL DOBBS

"Successive generations of proletarian revolutionists have participated in the movements of the working class and its allies. . . . Marxists today owe them not only homage for their deeds. We also have a duty to learn what they did wrong as well as right so their errors are not repeated." —*Farrell Dobbs*. Two volumes, $17 each.

Lenin's Final Fight

Speeches and Writings, 1922–23

V.I. LENIN

In 1922 and 1923, V.I. Lenin, central leader of the world's first socialist revolution, waged what was to be his last political battle—one that was lost after his death. At stake was whether that revolution, and the international communist movement it led, would remain on the revolutionary proletarian course that brought workers and peasants to power in October 1917. $17. Also in Spanish, Farsi, Greek.

The Transitional Program for Socialist Revolution

LEON TROTSKY

The Socialist Workers Party program, drafted by Trotsky in 1938, still guides the SWP and communists the world over. The party "uncompromisingly gives battle to all political groupings tied to the apron strings of the bourgeoisie. Its task—the abolition of capitalism's domination. Its aim—socialism. Its method—the proletarian revolution." $17. Also in Farsi.

Their Trotsky and Ours

JACK BARNES

To lead the working class in a successful revolution, a mass proletarian party is needed whose cadres, well beforehand, have absorbed a world communist program, are proletarian in life and work, derive deep satisfaction from doing politics, and have forged a leadership with an acute sense of what to do next. This book is about building such a party. $12. Also in Spanish, French, Farsi.

The Founding of the Socialist Workers Party

Minutes and Resolutions, 1938–39

JAMES P. CANNON

At founding gatherings of the Socialist Workers Party in 1938–39, revolutionists in the US codified two decades of experience in building a communist party. They charted a working-class course in resisting the coming imperialist war, fighting fascism and Jew-hatred, the struggle for Black rights, forging an alliance with exploited farmers, and the battle to transform the unions into revolutionary instruments of struggle by working people. $23

The Low Point of Labor Resistance Is Behind Us

The Socialist Workers Party Looks Forward

JACK BARNES
MARY-ALICE WATERS
STEVE CLARK

The global order imposed by Washington after its victory in World War II is shattering. A long retreat by the working class and unions has come to an end. The bosses and their government are stepping up attacks on our wages, conditions, and constitutional rights. This book highlights opportunities for building a mass proletarian party able to lead the struggle to end capitalist rule, opening a socialist future for humanity. $10. Also in Spanish and French.

Also from Pathfinder

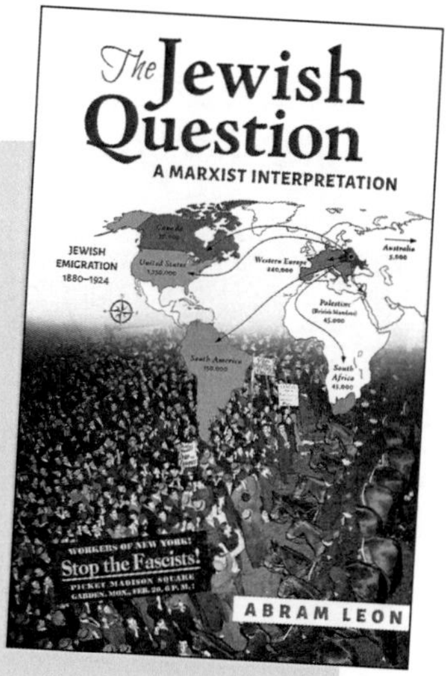

The Jewish Question

A MARXIST INTERPRETATION

Abram Leon

The battle against reactionary forces aiming to exterminate the Jews remains central to world politics, as shown by the genocidal October 2023 pogrom in Israel. Why is Jew-hatred still raising its ugly head? What are its class roots?

Why, as Abram Leon explains, is there no solution "independent of the world proletarian revolution"? Revised translation, new introduction, and 40 pages of illustrations and maps. $17. Also in Spanish and French.

The Communist Manifesto

Karl Marx and Frederick Engels

Communism, say the founding leaders of the revolutionary workers movement, is not a set of ideas or preconceived "principles" but workers' line of march to power, springing from a "movement going on under our very eyes." $5. Also in Spanish, French, Farsi, Arabic.

The Teamster Series

Farrell Dobbs

Four books on the strikes, organizing drives, and political campaigns that transformed the Teamsters across the Midwest in the 1930s into a militant industrial union movement. Written by Farrell Dobbs, the general organizer of these Teamster battles and leader of the Socialist Workers Party.

A tool for workers seeking to use union power in every workplace and advance the fight for an independent labor party. $16 each, series $50. Also in Spanish. *Teamster Rebellion* is also available in French, Farsi, Greek.

Malcolm X Talks to Young People

"The young generation of whites, Blacks, browns, whatever else—you're living at a time of revolution," said Malcolm in 1964. "And I for one will join with anyone, I don't care what color you are, as long as you want to change this miserable condition that exists on this earth." Four talks and an interview in the last months of Malcolm's life. $12. Also in Spanish, French, Farsi, Greek.

New International

A MAGAZINE OF MARXIST POLITICS AND THEORY

OPENING GUNS OF WORLD WAR III: WASHINGTON'S ASSAULT ON IRAQ

JACK BARNES

The murderous assault on Iraq in 1990–91 heralded increasingly sharp conflicts among imperialist powers, growing instability of capitalism, and more wars. Also includes:

1945: When US Troops Said No!
by Mary-Alice Waters

Lessons from the Iran-Iraq War
by Samad Sharif

In *New International* no. 7. $14. Also in Spanish, French, Farsi.

CAPITALISM'S LONG HOT WINTER HAS BEGUN

JACK BARNES

Today's global capitalist crisis is but the opening stage of decades of economic, financial, and social convulsions and class battles. Class-conscious workers confront this historic turning point for imperialism with confidence, Jack Barnes writes, drawing satisfaction from being "in their face" as we chart a revolutionary course to take power. In *New International* no. 12. $14. Also in Spanish, French, Farsi, Arabic, Greek.

U.S. IMPERIALISM HAS LOST THE COLD WAR

JACK BARNES

The collapse of regimes across Eastern Europe and the USSR claiming to be communist did not mean workers and farmers there had been crushed. In today's sharpening class conflicts and wars, these toilers are joining working people the world over in the class struggle against capitalist exploitation. In *New International* no. 11. $14. Also in Spanish, French, Farsi, Greek.

Labor, Nature, and the Evolution of Humanity

THE LONG VIEW OF HISTORY

Frederick Engels, Karl Marx
George Novack
Mary-Alice Waters

Without understanding that social labor, transforming nature, has driven humanity's evolution for millions of years, working people are unable to see beyond the capitalist epoch of class exploitation that warps all human relations, ideas, and values. Only the revolutionary conquest of state power by the working class can open the door to a world free of capitalist exploitation, degradation of nature, subjugation of women, racism, and war. A world built on human solidarity. A socialist world. $12. Also in Spanish and French.

50 Years of Covert Operations in the US

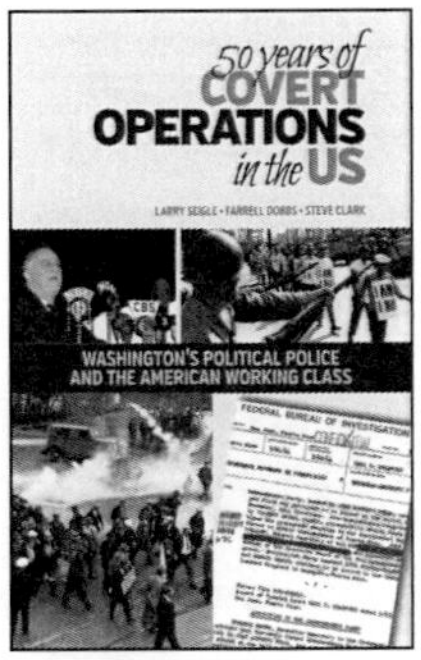

WASHINGTON'S POLITICAL POLICE AND THE AMERICAN WORKING CLASS

Larry Seigle, Farrell Dobbs
Steve Clark

How class-conscious workers have defended constitutional freedoms and fought the capitalists' drive to build the "national security" state essential to maintaining their rule. $10. Also in Spanish and Farsi.

Cosmetics, Fashions, and the Exploitation of Women

Joseph Hansen, Evelyn Reed
Mary-Alice Waters

How big business reinforces women's second-class status and uses it to rake in profits. Where does women's oppression come from? How has the entry of millions of women into the workforce strengthened the battle for emancipation, still to be won? $12. Also in Spanish, Farsi, Greek.

EXPAND YOUR REVOLUTIONARY LIBRARY

New edition!

Che Guevara on Economics and Politics in the Transition to Socialism

CARLOS TABLADA

It's essential for working people to win state power, said Ernesto Che Guevara. "Then there's the second stage, maybe more difficult than the first"—the transition from dog-eat-dog capitalism to socialism. That includes moving from work as a condition for survival, to voluntary social labor through which we express our common humanity. Includes Fidel Castro's 1987 speech "Che's Ideas are Absolutely Relevant Today." New edition with substantially expanded selections from Guevara's writings. $17. Also in Spanish, coming in French.

Leon Trotsky on France

An assessment of the social and economic crisis that shook France in the mid-1930s in the aftermath of Hitler's rise to power in Germany, and a program to unite the working class and exploited peasantry to confront it. $17

Socialism on Trial

Testimony at Minneapolis Sedition Trial

JAMES P. CANNON

The revolutionary program of the working class, presented in response to frame-up charges of "seditious conspiracy" in 1941, on the eve of US entry into World War II. The defendants were leaders of the Minneapolis labor movement and the Socialist Workers Party. $15. Also in Spanish, French, Farsi.

Thomas Sankara Speaks

The Burkina Faso Revolution, 1983–87

Under Sankara's guidance, Burkina Faso's revolutionary government led peasants, workers, women, and youth to expand literacy; to sink wells, plant trees, erect housing; to combat women's oppression; to carry out land reform; to join others worldwide to free themselves from the imperialist yoke. $20. Also in French.

Women in Cuba: The Making of a Revolution within the Revolution

VILMA ESPÍN, ASELA DE LOS SANTOS
YOLANDA FERRER

The integration of women in the ranks and leadership of the Cuban Revolution was intertwined with the proletarian course of the leadership of the revolution from the start. This is the story of that revolution and how it transformed the women and men who made it. $17. Also in Spanish, Farsi, Greek.

Colombia: Fidel Castro on the Debate around Revolutionary Strategy and Lessons of the Cuban Revolution

FROM THE PAGES OF THE *MILITANT*

Fidel Castro describes the Cuban leadership's efforts to end decades of war between the FARC guerrilla movement and Colombia's brutal regime. He explains why Cuban revolutionaries, unlike FARC leaders, rejected taking hostages and organized Cuba's working people to win state power, not pursue a "prolonged people's war." $5. Also in Spanish.

Pathfinder Press **accessible ebooks** for the blind, those with low vision, or other challenges reading print books

For a list of current accessible titles, go to: pathfinderpress.com/collections/books-for-the-blind.

Visit bookshare.org for information on how to sign up.

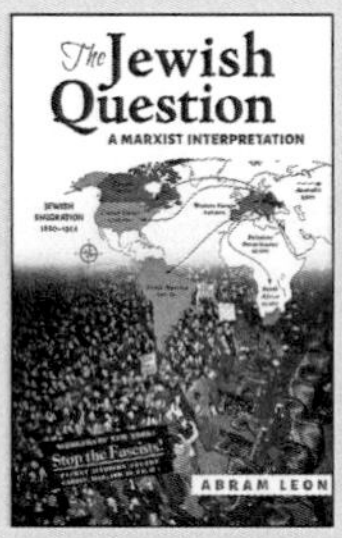